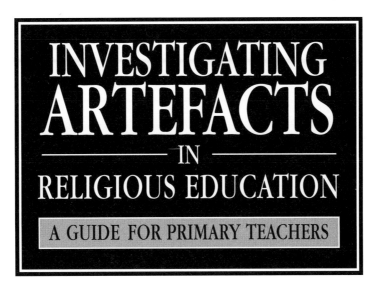

INVESTIGATING ARTEFACTS
IN
RELIGIOUS EDUCATION
A GUIDE FOR PRIMARY TEACHERS

CHRISTINE HOWARD

RMEP

RELIGIOUS AND MORAL EDUCATION PRESS

Religious and Moral Education Press
A division of SCM-Canterbury
Press Ltd, which is a subsidiary of Hymns Ancient & Modern Ltd
St Mary's Works, St Mary's Plain
Norwich, Norfolk NR3 3BH

First published 1995
Reprinted 2000
ISBN 1 85175-062-2

DEDICATION
To Mum and Dad with love and thanks.

ACKNOWLEDGEMENTS
I have always maintained that an effective advisory teacher is one who can recognize good ideas and communicate them to others. The world of RE is fortunate in having many advisers, inspectors, advisory teachers and classroom practitioners who are prepared to share their wisdom with others. In this regard I would like to say a special word of tribute to Vida Barnett, who can make artefacts come alive like no-one else and who has been a source of inspiration not only to me but to countless students and teachers of RE.

I am constantly amazed at how often human minds run in parallel, so that what I had thought was a new approach crops up somewhere else quite independently. A case of 'Great minds ...' or 'Fools seldom ...'? In writing this book I have not consciously copied anybody else's ideas, but I am aware that many of the techniques and approaches mentioned are already being used in classrooms throughout the country. That fact itself vouches for the value and efficacy of the methodology.

I am indebted to teachers throughout Britain whose suggestions, ideas, problems and enthusiasm have added to my own personal understanding of the significance of artefacts in RE.

Finally, I would like to thank my husband, Leslie, for his support and encouragement. Without him this book would not have been written.   **CH**

Thanks also to Daniel Skinner, Jennie Egan, Victoria Say and Thomas Bovey, pupils of Silverton Primary School, for appearing in the cover photographs.

Designed and typeset by **Topics** — The Creative Partnership, Exeter
Cover photography by Michael Burton-Pye
Illustrations by Clive Wakfer
Printed in Great Britain by Polestar Wheatons Ltd, Exeter
for Religious and Moral Education Press, Norwich

CONTENTS

THE AIMS OF RELIGIOUS EDUCATION

The following aims of religious education reflect a broad consensus about the subject's educational rationale and purpose. Religious education should help pupils to
- acquire and develop knowledge and understanding of Christianity and the other principal religions represented in Great Britain;
- develop an understanding of the influence of beliefs, values and traditions on individuals, communities, societies and cultures;
- develop the ability to make reasoned and informed judgements about religious and moral issues, with reference to the teachings of the principal religions represented in Great Britain;
- enhance their spiritual, moral, cultural and social development by:
  - developing awareness of the fundamental questions of life raised by human experiences, and of how religious teachings can relate to them
  - responding to such questions with reference to the teachings and practices of religions, and to their own understanding and experience
  - reflecting on their own beliefs , values and experiences in the light of their study;
- develop a positive attitude towards other people, respecting their right to hold different beliefs from their own, and towards living in a society of diverse religions.

(SCAA Religious Education Model Syllabus 1, 1994, page 4)

1

INTRODUCTION

Why Use Artefacts in RE?

Religious education is concerned with living faiths. Good RE thus goes beyond *facts* about religion and explores the attitudes, beliefs, morality and understanding which underlie the practice of those faiths. Both SCAA Model Syllabuses (1994) reflect this in their summary of the aims of religious education (see opposite), which are based on a broad consensus on the educational rationale for RE. Similar aims can be found in most Agreed Syllabuses and the Scottish 5–14 Document.

In an ideal world, the best source for this exploration would be direct contact with adherents of each religion: meeting people for whom its beliefs and practices are a daily reality. In the classroom this approach can present difficulties, however. Speakers who are able to communicate effectively with children may not be available locally, and certainly cannot be present at all the relevant RE lessons. Visits to places of worship are another possibility, but again there will be constraints of time, money and local availability.

Other RE resources, however valuable, are always at least one remove from the believer. For example, videos can allow members of faith communities to speak through them but are not truly interactive. Although IT *can* be an interactive medium, and recent programs are beginning to explore exciting new avenues for RE, such resources are limited by what has been programmed into them. Religious artefacts, too, have their limitations but are nevertheless a powerful RE resource. The chart overleaf gives an idea of their potential.

Religious artefacts are items used by believers in the practice of their faith and can thus provide insights into their beliefs and attitudes. Some artefacts are not in themselves 'special' but, like a Qur'an stand (ra'el), serve a practical purpose. Others, however, represent a communication with the Divine and as such are sacred: for example, the Torah scrolls in Judaism.

Religious artefacts do not stand alone. They need to be interpreted. That is, they all have particular contexts and roles within the faith to which they belong. It is understanding the way in which artefacts are used or the purpose for which they are intended that takes the student beyond the object itself to a deeper awareness of the religious concepts which lie behind it.

Religious artefacts can be used in a wide variety of ways to enrich the teaching environment. For example, they appeal to the senses and can excite children's interest. This book introduces several different approaches to using artefacts in RE and gives detailed examples of how each method could be applied to specific objects. It is hoped that this will stimulate teachers to explore and develop the use of artefacts in their own classrooms. Imaginative teachers can see many different ways to encourage pupils in their search for meaning and understanding in RE. Use of artefacts will, of course, stand alongside other teaching techniques involving books or other resources such as those mentioned above.

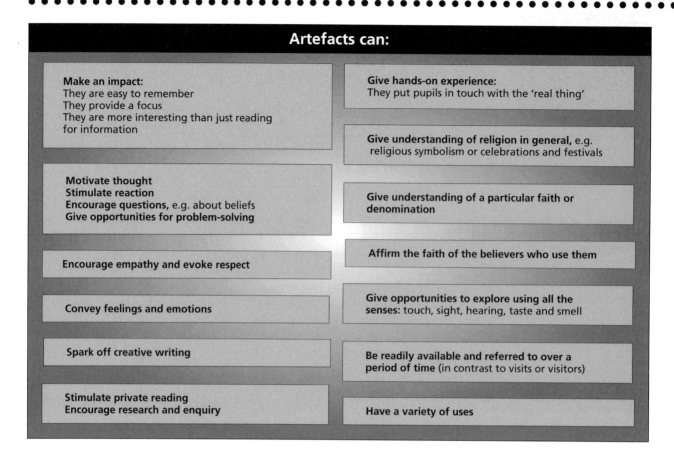

Artefacts can:

Make an impact:
They are easy to remember
They provide a focus
They are more interesting than just reading for information

Give hands-on experience:
They put pupils in touch with the 'real thing'

Give understanding of religion in general, e.g. religious symbolism or celebrations and festivals

Motivate thought
Stimulate reaction
Encourage questions, e.g. about beliefs
Give opportunities for problem-solving

Give understanding of a particular faith or denomination

Encourage empathy and evoke respect

Affirm the faith of the believers who use them

Convey feelings and emotions

Give opportunities to explore using all the senses: touch, sight, hearing, taste and smell

Spark off creative writing

Be readily available and referred to over a period of time (in contrast to visits or visitors)

Stimulate private reading
Encourage research and enquiry

Have a variety of uses

How to Find Your Way Round This Book

CHAPTER 2 gives general guidance on the wide range of possible classroom activities involving religious artefacts, on how to ensure that artefact activities deliver RE effectively and on how to tackle areas of sensitivity.

CHAPTERS 3–8 each explore a different approach to using artefacts and follow a similar pattern. After an introduction to the approach, an example of how it might be put into practice using one or more specific artefacts is described in detail. This plan for a lesson or series of lessons includes aims and indicates some of the learning processes and skills which pupils can thus develop. It also lists the resources which will be needed if the plan is followed in its entirety and gives ideas for follow-up work. Where appropriate, additional background information on the artefacts is provided and any areas of sensitivity which might need to be addressed are pointed out. Other ways of using the approach, with artefacts from different faiths, are suggested along with some back-up resources.

Finally, each of these chapters includes a short story linked to the RE content of the sample lesson(s). This could be either read as part of the school day or used in a follow-up act of collective worship.

CHAPTER 9 gives advice on how to build up your own collection of religious artefacts. It provides examples of basic collections for each of the six main world faiths and suggests how these might be used. It also looks at thematic collections and includes a story.

RESOURCE LIST: This suggests general resources supporting the use of artefacts in the classroom.

INDEX: This includes page references for all the religious artefacts mentioned in the book as well as key issues such as sensitivity. Entries for religious terms which may be unfamiliar to some readers also indicate where these are explained in the text.

2 POSSIBILITIES AND PREVENTING PROBLEMS

What Are Religious Artefacts?

Strictly speaking, an artefact is 'a thing made by human workmanship' *(Chambers Twentieth Century Dictionary)*. In RE, however, the term 'religious artefact' is generally extended to cover any object which is used in the practice of religion, including naturally occurring items and religious pictures or texts. This broader definition, which will also be adopted here, allows all of the following examples to be classed as religious artefacts:

- A conch shell, used in Hindu worship, or a shofar, a ram's horn blown in Judaism at Rosh Hashanah (New Year) and Yom Kippur (Day of Atonement)
- A woven garland of flowers, used to decorate a murti (statue) of a deity or worn in celebration
- A religious picture, especially when it represents something beyond itself, e.g. a picture of a Hindu deity or a Christian icon
- A woven hanging or scroll with a religious theme
- A framed quotation from a religious text, e.g. the Qur'an
- A book, particularly a sacred text

NOTE: Although many 'Old Masters' on religious themes are not strictly religious artefacts, they are nevertheless a rich source of symbolism and atmosphere. They can also tell us something of the time and people who painted them and can be contrasted dramatically with more-modern renderings of the same theme.

How Do Religious Artefacts Differ from Other Objects?

Religious artefacts are different because they are intended for use in a religious context. They may be used as part of a religious ritual or as a support to worship or belief. For example, a religious artefact may act as a focal point for meditation or may simply have a practical function in worship.

Religious artefacts are the *actual* objects used in a religion itself and may symbolize an important religious concept or truth. Some may go beyond this and become part of a reality which they are representing. For example, according to Roman Catholic belief, the bread and wine at Mass is transformed at the moment of consecration into the body and blood of Christ, so that the communicant who receives it becomes one with his or her crucified Redeemer. In some, though by no means all cases, an artefact may serve as a means of communication between worshippers and the Divine.

How special religious artefacts are *in themselves* varies considerably. For example, Shabbat (Jewish Sabbath) candlesticks are, at the end of the day, just candlesticks with a practical purpose. In themselves, they have no religious significance. What is important is the context in which they are used, namely the welcoming every Friday evening of Shabbat, the day of rest ordained by God. Similarly, some aids to worship such as prayer-beads or bells are not special in themselves.

Other artefacts become special by association. For example, in some parts of India the turban is a common form of headgear worn by Hindus and Muslims as well as Sikhs. Yet when worn by a Sikh to keep his long uncut hair in place (as commanded by Guru Gobind Singh), a turban takes on a religious significance: it becomes special by association.

Finally, there are religious artefacts which are always special. The technical term for these is 'sacred' or 'holy', meaning something which is set aside. These sacred objects are set aside for use only in communication with the Divine. In certain branches of Christianity this is represented by the sanctuary (the section of a church containing the altar) and its furniture. No-one but the priests and those specially chosen are allowed to enter the sanctuary, the underlying reason here being fear of contamination of the holy by the profane. The holy books of some other religions, notably the Torah scrolls in Judaism and the Qur'an in Islam, fall into this category because, for many believers, they contain words communicated directly by God (see Chapter 5). This means that having some religious artefacts in the classroom (for use in a non-religious albeit educational way) is not appropriate, e.g. full-size, handwritten Torah scrolls. In other cases, it means knowing how to handle the artefact, e.g. a copy of the Qur'an, as members of the faith would have it treated.

In schools, all religious artefacts should always be treated with respect by pupils and teachers. It is essential to do this in order not to cause offence to faith members. It is also an important way of helping children to appreciate the significance of the artefacts and/or the religious context in which they are used by believers.

For more details on handling artefacts, see pages 11–13.

How Can Artefacts Be Used in RE?

The diagram opposite lists a whole variety of ways in which religious artefacts can be used in the classroom. It is a collation of the results of brainstorming by many groups of teachers from all over the UK. It does not claim to be an exhaustive list and I have not tried to 'unpack' each suggestion. What the list does is to give a glimpse of the wide range of activities in which artefacts can be used. Chapters 3–8 explore some of these approaches and describe in detail sample activities involving particular religious artefacts. There are, however, a few general points which teachers need to bear in mind when planning artefact activities for their own pupils.

1. Not all activities involving religious artefacts are in themselves RE.
Just because the children make a Torah scroll or draw a Hindu deity or eat karah parshad, for example, it doesn't mean they are automatically 'doing' RE.

Making a Torah scroll may be CDT or art, but it becomes RE only when the children discuss questions such as why the scrolls are on wooden rollers (the staff of life), what are appropriate symbols for decorating the mantle and what those symbols mean, why it would be inappropriate to use passages from the New Testament inside the scrolls or why people shouldn't be drawn on them (do not make graven images).

A good test for RE content is to ask:

- Does the activity explore the symbols on or in the artefact?
- Does it help explain the meaning of the artefact?
- Does it explore the way in which the artefact is used by believers?
- Does it encourage understanding of the way in which the artefact is regarded within the faith and hence respect for it?

Possibilities for Using Artefacts

- For information/explanation

- For greater understanding

- In matching exercises

- For asking questions, e.g. 'What is it for?' (i.e. problem-solving)

- In brainstorming

- For research or investigation

- For revision or to reinforce learning

- As a stimulus or to create interest
  See Chapter 3

- As subjects for or to stimulate discussion

- To introduce a topic or idea
  See Chapter 3

- In exploring patterns and symbols
  See Chapter 4

- For permanent or temporary display
  See Chapter 6

- To encourage respect

- To develop empathy

- To encourage appreciation of beauty, art, etc.
  See page 61

- To engender appreciation of the love, care and skill that went into making the artefact and what the artefact means or represents to the believer

- In estimation (Maths), e.g. monetary value, weight

- To make comparisons and contrasts
  See Chapter 4

- In drama and role-play
  See Chapter 7

- In demonstrations
  See Chapter 7 for more explanation, including do's and don'ts

- As objects to make in art and craft work

- As objects to spot on a video

- For observation and drawing

- In the home corner or, in some cases (e.g. dreidle), in play
  See also pages 13 –14

- To stimulate the senses: taste, smell, hearing, as well as touch and sight

- As something to cook (and taste!)

- To raise environmental and economic issues

- To encourage listening and responding

- To create visual impact, a stimulating and exciting atmosphere or a peaceful and reflective atmosphere

- To aid reflection or as a focus

- To explore the affective area
  See Chapter 8 for more explanation, including do's and don'ts

- In collective worship

- For stilling

- To stimulate creative writing, imagination, poetry, story-telling

- As the starting-point of a guided fantasy

- As a link with story, myth and poetry

- In collaborative group work

- In individual work

- Does it point beyond the artefact itself to the beliefs of the religious tradition?
- Does it encourage the children to ask 'ultimate questions', including questions of morality?
- Does it aid the children's understanding of the search for meaning in life which is common to humankind?

If the activity contributes to one or more of these areas then it can be legitimately classed as RE. At the end of the day it is not the artefact itself that is important but the religious concepts or beliefs to which it points.

2. Remember that religious artefacts need explanation.
Artefacts are a wonderful way of getting children to ask questions, to explore religious objects and their meanings, and to use as a jumping-off point for further research. Nevertheless, we must always remember that religious artefacts can't talk! Children will need help in interpreting them and understanding the religious context in which they are used. This means that lessons involving artefacts need to be carefully prepared with plenty of additional resources to aid the learning process, such as videos, tapes, books, photographs, visits or visitors – in other words, the normal spread of teaching techniques.

It is important to remember also that not only will some items be unfamiliar but the context in which they are used by believers or the ideas which they represent may be beyond the children's experience. Teachers may therefore need to devise 'ways in' to help children understand their significance. The introductory activity on page 35 is an example of how a child's understanding of special or favourite books can be used as a 'way in' to the concept of holy books. Some families may have 'best china' which is used for important family occasions or special guests and this can link in with Pesach (Passover) crockery. The principle here is to move from the familiar and known within the child's experience and understanding to that which is unfamiliar and new. (See also point 3 on page 12).

3. Not all religious groups use artefacts as much as others.
There are often differences here between denominations and sects within the same religion as well as between different faiths. In Non-conformist Christian denominations such as the Baptist Church, statues are not generally found because of the reaction against 'idol worship' which stemmed from the Reformation in the sixteenth century. Similar attitudes can be found in Orthodox Judaism and are also central to Islam. In Sikhism, too, there is a growing tendency for statues of the ten Gurus to be considered unacceptable. It is interesting to contrast these attitudes with those of the Roman Catholic Church and of Hinduism and Buddhism, where statues, murtis or rupas, for many, form an integral part of religious expression.

Both the use and the lack of artefacts can give insight into a faith. It is important, however, to choose artefacts for the classroom that accurately reflect the religion being represented. Some apparently interesting and attractive items may play a tiny, insignificant role and would give the wrong impression of the faith as a whole. Artefacts important to particular (sizeable) denominations may be suitable provided that it is made clear to pupils that not all members of that faith use or, necessarily, approve of them. Not all Roman Catholics use rosary-beads, for example, and there is a variety of practice in the wearing of kippahs in Judaism. Some Muslim women will wear Western-style clothes as long as they are modest, whilst others cover their arms, legs and head at all times, and so on.

**How Can Religious
Artefacts Be Handled?**

When I'm leading in-service training sessions on artefacts, teachers almost always ask me questions relating to issues of sensitivity in handling and storage. Drawing up a list of do's and don'ts which covered every eventuality would be difficult, if not impossible since within any religion there is a variety of opinion about what can and can't be done. Many people are aware that this is the case in Christianity, with its plethora of denominations, but overlook the fact that similar diversity is found in other religions as well. Moreover, what might be unacceptable in one context might be all right in another.

In the following chapters, I shall point out some of the most obvious areas where issues of sensitivity are most strongly felt. Meanwhile, here are a few basic ground rules to help teachers make their own judgements within their own school and community context.

1. Do always treat all religious artefacts with respect at all times.
Many artefacts have a special meaning to the members of the faith that use them. Their feelings should be respected. Some artefacts should be treated in particular ways: for example, the Qur'an should always be kept off the ground with nothing placed on top of it. (See also Chapter 5.) In other cases, however, showing respect means simply remembering that the artefacts are 'special' and should be treated with care, not as sources of amusement.

Other members of staff also need to be sensitized to showing respect – though this may be more difficult than with children! Respect needs to extend beyond the classroom, too. Children are quick to spot inconsistencies in our behaviour and attitudes: 'Actions speak louder than words'. It's no good showing respect for artefacts, and insisting that children do the same, if as soon as bell goes and the children have left the room, all instructions about handling and storage observed with such care five minutes before are ignored and, for example, the Qur'an is dumped in a box on the storeroom floor with other boxes on top of it.

Some people have suggested that it doesn't matter if faith members are not aware of what is happening as long as we treat artefacts properly in front of the children. I disagree. It seems to me akin to saying that we can make sexist or racist remarks so long as we don't do so in front of the children, and there is no-one of the opposite sex or race in question present!

The issue is not one of belief in the artefact or its religious context itself. It is one of respect for the beliefs and feelings of others. We have to remember that members of the faith communities trust teachers in this regard and are generally happy to support them in their work. We shall forfeit this trust and support if true respect is lacking.

To some teachers this approach may appear to be foolish, oversensitive and unwarranted, or it may conflict with their own beliefs, whether these are religious or not. If they are in all conscience unable to handle artefacts with sensitivity and respect, it may be possible for them to arrange for another member of staff or a child belonging to the faith, should there be one in the class, to demonstrate an artefact or holy book.

There are cases where the teaching of RE raises real crises of conscience for some, because certain beliefs held by others are regarded as wrong or offensive. Examples might be a Christian handling murtis (statues) of Hindu deities or showing respect to the Qur'an, or a Jewish teacher talking about the Resurrection of Jesus. It is hard to see how a teacher who felt that his or her own beliefs would be compromised in these or similar circumstances could present *any* faith objectively or exhibit proper respect for the beliefs of others.

It is unlikely that good multifaith RE is going to take place in that classroom and I would suggest that the teacher seriously considers exercising the right to withdraw, for everyone's sake.

2. Do listen to the local community.

The SCAA Model Syllabuses for RE (1994) have helped to produce a national consensus about what should be covered in each of the major faiths listed in the Education Reform Act 1988. However, responsibility for the balance and nitty-gritty of what is taught in county schools and how it is approached still lies with the local faith communities through their official mouthpieces, the Agreed Syllabus Conference and Standing Advisory Council for Religious Education, or SACRE. If you have any doubts or problems concerning the suitability of what is being done with artefacts in your school, your local SACRE is a useful body for reference. It is most easily approached through the local authority's advisory teacher for RE (who is often a fount of all knowledge to do with RE!) or the inspector for RE. Church schools should first approach their Diocesan Board of Education, as their requirements may be slightly different. Local RE centres are also often a useful source of information and able to give helpful advice.

Do listen to parents and local religious leaders but remember that there is a variety of opinion amongst religious communities themselves about what is and isn't appropriate. An individual's view of their religion and of religious education may not be representative of the faith as a whole. For example, some Sikhs do not approve of made-up, starched turbans and beard-nets, others accept them as useful aids in a busy world, a type of labour-saving device. Similarly, some Christians (e.g. many Roman Catholics) see statues as an integral part of the expression of their faith, whilst others (mainly from Non-conformist traditions) see them as a violation of the First Commandment: 'You shall not make any graven image'. Hence official bodies and trained RE advisers may need to be consulted to achieve balance and perspective.

3. Do avoid an approach to using artefacts which plays on the exotic or curiosity angle.

It is tempting to present an artefact to children as something strange or weird, even, as this awakens interest and stimulates imagination. Unfortunately, doing this may also create in the children's minds the wrong type of image of the religion of which it is part and the believers who use it.

Many religious artefacts may indeed be unfamiliar to pupils, but questions which draw out links with similar artefacts that pupils have encountered in a different, maybe secular context will help to overcome the strangeness problem. For example, you could ask:

- Do you or any of your friends or family have one of these?
- Have you seen one before or anything like it?
- Where did you see it?
- What is it used for?
- What might it be used for?

4. Do handle all sacred texts with care and respect.

For more information about the issues involved and procedures for handling and storing sacred texts, see Chapter 5.

5. Do avoid giving the impression that Hindus 'worship statues' (or, worse, 'idols').

The correct term for a statue of a Hindu deity is 'murti', meaning 'form'. Murtis in the home and mandir (temple) are treated with very great respect (i.e. venerated) as *representations* of the deities, forms of the Supreme Spirit, or God. Calling a murti a 'statue' may cause offence.

6. Whenever sacred books or artefacts are used in the context of an act of worship, those organizing it should be aware of any possible causes of offence which might arise.
For example, it would not be appropriate to bring the Qur'an into the room during the singing of a Christian hymn.

7. Do enjoy teaching RE!
When many teachers have to take RE seriously for the first time, they are so put off by what they see as problems (generally arising from a lack of knowledge or training in this area) that they fail to see the possibilities. Good RE touches on every aspect of life: the rituals with which we mark the important events of our lives; the festivals which punctuate the rhythm of the seasons and give us pauses in the daily pattern of life; the basic need that humans have to search for a meaning to life; the moral codes by which we live; the historical origins of many of our institutions; the shape of the global map; our understanding of world politics; great works of art, literature and music; how we relate to others, and what shapes our view of the world.

Primary-aged children are eager to explore the religious dimension in life, unfettered by the doubts and scepticism of teenage and adult years. It can be a privilege and joy to learn with them.

Artefacts and Key Stage 1

Teachers of younger children often express concern about using religious artefacts. Their fear is that proper respect will be lacking in a world where everything is 'hands on'. This very fact can be turned to advantage, however.

Before any artefact is introduced the children can be prepared. The concept of specialness is one which even the youngest children can grasp. They could be encouraged to talk about things which are special to them or to their families, why they are special, how they would feel if someone touched something special to them, or took it without permission or damaged it in any way. How would it make them feel if someone laughed at them because of its specialness? This provides a link to religious artefacts, which are special objects to believers.

Many aspects of infant RE can be approached through the concept of specialness: special days (days of worship); special holidays (festivals); special buildings (places of worship); special books (sacred writings); special people (religious leaders). The term 'special' is almost the secular equivalent of the religious term 'holy' or 'sacred', meaning 'set aside'. However, not all religious artefacts are special in this sense. Some are everyday objects, such as Shabbat (Sabbath) candlesticks, which could be any candle-holder. The specialness comes from the use to which they are put.

Safety

The safety aspect must be considered with all pupils but particularly with very young children. Religious artefacts (with a very few exceptions) are not toys and are not designed for young children to handle. Some may be quite crudely made and may have sharp edges or nasty points, others may contain lead paint. This is because they are the *actual* articles used by believers. They belong to the adult world and reflect the background and conditions of the place where they were made. It is therefore advisable to check all artefacts for suitability before letting the children handle them.

Where there are toys which are made for children belonging to a faith, such as the 'Touch Torah' range of soft-toy artefacts produced specifically for Jewish children, there should be no problem. However, don't be misled by manufacturers' descriptions. For example, not all 'dolls' are suitable for playing with. Some are strictly for display only.

A few 'real' artefacts are designed to be played with, e.g. the dreidle. That is their religious context. However, it might not be appropriate to 'play' with some other artefacts, even if children could do so safely. This may have implications for a home corner. Should we include some artefacts associated with religion? If so how, and which ones are appropriate? For example, if the class were studying Judaism, would it be all right to make a 'Jewish' home corner, perhaps with a mezuzah and with the table set for Shabbat (Sabbath)? Opinions on this issue vary amongst RE inspectors and advisers. Personally, I think that as long as the children are aware of the religious context and the home corner is integrated into the study of the religion, with the children being taught proper respect for the artefacts and their use, it is probably an acceptable learning experience akin to role-play with older children.

Artefacts and Special Needs

It is impossible to do justice to the challenges presented by Special Needs children here. Those needs are so wide that it is nonsense to group them all together under one umbrella heading. Having said that, there is no doubt that artefacts provide an ideal approach for many Special Needs pupils. This is because they are essentially a 'hands on', experiential, concrete but not content-laden type of resource, i.e. artefacts are open ended in terms of the amount of knowledge which is associated with them in a particular activity. They can be used without prior knowledge and the teacher can directly control any learning approaches and outcomes.

Thus artefacts can be selected and activities adapted for use with a broad band of children. A blind child can touch and smell and hear; a deaf child can feel and see and taste. An older child with learning disabilities will not be confronted with something patently designed for a young child and an able child will have a range of possibilities to explore.

Two areas which do need to be highlighted in planning a Special Needs strategy are:

- How should the issue of respect and sensitivity be handled with children who have severe behavioural difficulties? There may well be a tension here between the hands-on approach and the great respect which we should show to some religious artefacts. In these cases, the teacher might choose a 'look but don't touch' approach, keeping the artefact under his or her own control. Sometimes handling the artefact could be a reward for achievement or good behaviour. Sometimes it may be felt that it is not appropriate to use the most sensitive artefacts in that particular situation at that time. The final decision has to be left to the teacher, who will be able to judge what is appropriate.
- As with very young children, addressing the safety aspects will be important.

Artefacts and Stories

Story has always been an important element in religion. We need only to look at some of the great religious teachers to appreciate this. Where, for example, would the Gospels be without the stories (parables) Jesus told? Thus it is not surprising that story and stories form an important part of RE also. Colin Wilkinson puts it like this:

A 'good' story, either read or heard, will help the reader or listener to see, think, feel, experience and possibly understand at least something of its characters. In so doing the reader or listener's experience will be widened and deepened. In the context of RE and its key concepts, stories illuminate both the basic human experience and the basic patterns that are common to all religions.

(*Religion and Story*. Article in *World Religions in Education 1990–91*, published by Shap)

When we start to relate artefacts to story in RE we add a further dimension. Many stories can begin with a focus on an artefact. Alternatively the artefact itself may have arisen out of a story. Consider a statue of Our Lady of Lourdes. Her bearing, the rosary she carries and the flowers at her feet, all have their place within the story of her revelation to the young servant girl Bernadette. This story is common to all statues of Our Lady of Lourdes. Yet individual examples may have their own particular story too. For example, the statue may have been purchased from the shrine at Lourdes by a visiting pilgrim. The artefact then embraces a whole new story which is peculiar to itself. For the development of the use of story and artefacts, the series *A Gift to the Child* (see page 77) provides an interesting approach.

Many teachers are avid collectors of artefacts. They pick up bargains, they buy artefacts from abroad when on holiday, they are given presents of artefacts. Often there is a personal story attached, either to the gift or the giver. They may have bargained for the artefact, they may have hunted it down in an out-of-the-way place or been involved in a long, arduous search for a particular artefact. These stories add interest and meaning to the artefacts we use.

Because of the importance of story in RE and its obvious links with artefacts, I have included a related story at the end of each chapter. These can be used in a variety of ways, depending on the needs of the teacher and pupils. The following are a few suggestions to get you started.

The stories could be used:

- during a quiet/story time at the beginning or end of the day;
- integrated into a scheme of work;
- to introduce an artefact;
- to reinforce ideas developed in lessons;
- as discussion starters;
- as a starting-point for drama or role-play;
- as an element in an act of collective worship.

The stories included here come from different backgrounds. Some are based on historical events, some belong to the class of writing described as mythology, some are purely fictional. As with the artefacts, it is hoped that teachers will enjoy using these stories – and others of their own – and find them a springboard for exploring story, artefacts and RE further.

3 THE STIMULUS OR 'KEYHOLE' APPROACH

Artefacts are an ideal way to introduce a new topic or new area within a religion. They give 'hands-on' experience and are a wonderful way of exciting children's interest and engaging them in questioning. The questions can lead on to investigation and research as the children set about finding some of the answers for themselves.

For best effect in these circumstances, the artefacts should be presented singly or perhaps two at a time at most. The more active the presentation, the better it will be remembered and the more questions will be asked.

Do's and Don'ts

Although this approach is deliberately designed to awaken children's interest, care should be taken to avoid artefacts that may appear too 'curious' or 'exotic', since this will have a negative effect on children's understanding of their religious significance. Some artefacts, if introduced without proper preparation, may invoke laughter, even ridicule or perhaps distaste. For example, some children may find a made-up starched turban strange, others may dislike the bright colours typical of many images of Hindu deities. Another response might be: 'What would they want to do that for?' or 'That's silly.' Try to foresee areas where this might happen and forestall such reactions, introducing items only when you feel the children are ready to appreciate their importance and significance.

This means the artefacts should be chosen with thought and the ground prepared carefully. One of the aims of RE is to teach our pupils respect for other people and their beliefs and practices, but this does not just happen. We have to lay the foundations first. This can be done in a variety of ways: by discussion and pointing out parallels within the children's experience; by making materials from a wide variety of cultures available across the curriculum; above all, by the attitudes displayed and inculcated by the staff at all times.

The aim of the stimulus or keyhole approach is to introduce artefacts which open the way into a fuller exploration of the religions which employ them. These artefacts may or may not be special or significant in themselves. Their main RE purpose here is to attract the pupils' interest and to get them asking questions.

EXAMPLE: A Muslim Prayer-mat with Qiblah Compass

AIMS:
- To explore some of the main tenets of Islam.
- To encourage the children to ask questions themselves.
- To stimulate their interest.

The qiblah is the direction of the Ka'bah in the city of Makkah (Mecca), which all Muslims must face when performing salah (daily prayer). To find this direction, the qiblah compass is rotated until its magnetic needle points to the correct number for the country where the user is at the time. Most qiblah compasses come with a small booklet which gives the figures for every country in the world. In the UK this will be 250° (or 25° on some compasses). There will be another indicator or pointer on the compass, often in the form of a minaret, which then gives the direction of prayer.

It is a good idea to have a practice beforehand in the classroom where you intend to do the following activity so that you have a rough idea of the direction you and the mat will be facing. This speeds up the process and thus reduces the opportunity for restless behaviour.

Investigating a Muslim Prayer-mat with Qiblah Compass

Resources	Prayer-mat and qiblah compass. Some prayer-mats have a compass attached. If yours does not, a separate, hand-held compass will be needed.

Pupil Response	Activity
	Arrange the class so that everyone will be able to see what is happening. The children should be settled and quiet before the activity begins. The first part of the activity proceeds in silence and could be introduced with a sentence such as: 'Watch carefully what I am going to do as we are going to be asking some questions about it later.' If the class is used to this kind of approach an introduction might not be necessary.
Observing	Unroll the prayer-mat and place it on the floor. Use the compass to find the direction of the Ka'bah in Makkah and position the mat so that it is facing that way. Stand at the foot of the mat, facing the Ka'bah, for a few moments.
Asking questions Deductive reasoning	Turn to the class and develop the lesson using a 'Twenty Questions' format, challenging the children to discover who might normally do what you have just done and why. Tell them how many questions they are allowed to ask and that you will answer only 'Yes' or 'No'.
Cooperating Ranking	If the class is small enough, the pupils can decide collectively which questions to ask. Alternatively, the class could be divided into smaller groups which take it in turns to ask a question. Each group first decides on a list of questions and ranks them in order of priority. As each group will hear the answers given to questions from other groups, the number of questions allowed per group can be reduced from twenty as appropriate.
Listening Responding	At the end of the 'game', the children should have some idea about who uses the mat and what it is for. If not, explain briefly that it is a prayer-mat which a Muslim man or woman might use when praying and that this prayer is always done facing the Ka'bah in Makkah. This is obviously going to raise a lot more questions, which can be investigated in follow-up work.

Follow-up Activities

Because prayer is such a fundamental part of Islam, by studying just one aspect of it we can open up a whole area of knowledge about Muslim belief and practice. The chart opposite shows four possible areas which could be covered by following up the questions:

- **Who** uses the mat?
- **Why** does a Muslim pray?
- **How** does a Muslim pray?
- **What** is the compass for?

It is not suggested that each area is covered but one or two could be investigated, depending on the aspects of Islam included in the programmes of study for any particular group. There is in any case considerable overlap between the areas which could be approached via these four questions.

Additional Notes on Prayer-mats

Some Muslims argue that, with the exception of the Qur'an (see Chapter 5), artefacts in Islam have no special significance *in themselves*. Therefore a prayer-mat simply provides a clean area on which to pray. This practical requirement can easily be appreciated when one realizes that each rak'ah (unit of salah) involves prostration: touching the forehead and nose to the floor. Thus prayer-mats can be made of many different types of material, ranging from cheap bamboo mats of the sort holiday-makers use on the beach, through lightweight linen or cotton mats, through machine or handwoven mats of varying quality, to expensive Persian carpets. It is said that in the desert, a traveller may draw an area in the sand and use this for prayer.

Many prayer-mats have designs which incorporate a mihrab, the alcove or niche in a mosque wall indicating the direction of prayer. Others have representations of the Ka'bah in Makkah or the Prophet's Mosque in Madinah. Some suggest that these mats should be treated with respect because they are decorated with the holy places of Islam. Still others say that a prayer-mat should always be treated with respect, because when it is used for prayer it becomes a mosque.

In Islam, as in every other religion, a variety of opinion and interpretation can be found. One point on which all Muslims agree, however, is that prayer-mats, like mosques, should never be decorated with people, hence the development of the beautiful arabesque and geometric shapes that have adorned Islamic art over the centuries.

Who Uses the Mat?

A Muslim: someone who accepts Islam and can say the Shahadah:

'There is no god but Allah, Muhammad is the Messenger of Allah.'

- **Allah** … Arabic name for the One God … Muslims submit to the Will of Allah… Islam is the peace attained by so doing (cf. 'Shalom', the Hebrew word for 'peace')

- **Muhammad** (Peace be upon him) … last or seal of the Prophets … his life and call … revelation and importance of the Qur'an (see also Chapter 5)

How Does a Muslim Pray?

- **Preparations for prayer** … wudu (ritual washing) … removing shoes … covering head

- **Salah:** formal, prescribed daily prayer for all Muslims … five times a day … rak'ahs (sets of fixed postures and recitations in Arabic constituting salah) … symbol of Ummah (worldwide unity of Islam)

- **Du'a:** less formal, personal and intercessory prayer … often said at the end of salah… use of prayer-beads (subhah or tasbih)

- **Adhan:** call to prayer … from minaret … by mu'adhin (muezzin) … Bilal (see page 21)

- **Communal prayer:** Friday prayers at mosque … sermon by imam … men and women pray separately

- **Allah:** the One God to whom prayer is addressed

Why Does a Muslim Pray?

Prayer, in the form of salah, five times a day, is a religious duty, the second of the Five Pillars of Islam.

- **Shahadah** (declaration of faith) is the first Pillar of Islam …

- **Zakah:** almsgiving, the third Pillar of Islam … customary at the festival Eid-ul-Fitr

- **Sawm:** fasting, the fourth Pillar of Islam … Ramadan

- **Hajj:** pilgrimage to Makkah, the fifth Pillar of Islam … Eid-ul-Adha

- **Purpose of prayer** (older pupils only): for example, salah is regarded as a form of communication with and worship of Allah

What Is the Compass For?

To find the qiblah, the direction of the Ka'bah in Makkah.

- **Qiblah:** Muslims must face this way when perfoming salah … the mihrab (niche or alcove in wall) indicates this direction for communal prayer in the mosque … symbol of Ummah (worldwide unity of Islam)

- **Compass:** how it works … not required when Muslims are praying somewhere familiar, e.g. at home

- **Ka'bah:** the cube-shaped building and its covering … its significance as the first building for worship of the One True God … association with Ibrahim (Abraham) … Eid-ul-Adha

- **Makkah:** Hajj (pilgrimage) … Madinah (Medina)

Other Ideas for Using the Keyhole Approach

	Artefacts associated with prayer	Artefacts which could be used as stimulus for studying different topics
Buddhism	Prayer-wheel, prayer-flag, mala (prayer-beads) Note, however, that there is no concept of prayer in Buddhism in the sense that it is found in other religions, since Buddhists acknowledge no supreme power or deity to which to pray.	**Eight-spoked wheel** … Teachings of the Buddha … Four Noble Truths … Eightfold Path
Christianity	Rosary-beads	**Cross or crucifix** … Symbols of Christianity … Incarnation … Easter (death and resurrection) … Atonement
Hinduism	Mala (prayer-beads), prayer-shawl	**Shiva Nataraja** (Lord of the Dance) … Cycle of samsara (rebirth) and moksha (liberation from rebirth) … Brahma, Vishnu, Shiva (the Trimurti) … Brahman
Judaism	Tallit, tefillin	**Mezuzah** … Shema … Torah and its laws … Moses
Sikhism	Mala (prayer-beads)	**Nishan Sahib** (Sikh flag) … Unity of Khalsa … Five K's

STORY

Bilal Makes His First Call

No doubt there were more handsome buildings – none of us were architects – and I can't say that I've ever stood under the dome of the Church of the Holy Wisdom in Byzantium, but what we made, we made; a house within our worship. As we rested on the floor after our labours gazing up at the soft dappled light filtering through the palm thatch of the roof, Hamza had his own fine words for our handiwork: 'It's like the cradle of Moses,' he said, and the comparison pleased the Prophet. Indeed it was a cool place, refreshing to the spirit and pleasing to the eye, a green shade.

But although the Mosque was built, it was still incomplete.

It was Ali, I think, who told us it needed one more touch. 'We're missing something ... something high up there,' he said, pointing to the roof, 'some signal ... a way to call people in.'

'We could run a flag up,' suggested Ammar.

In a moment we were all going backwards and forwards, up and down, arguing how best to call the Faithful to their prayer. The Prophet sat through it all with his arms folded, neither taking himself out of or putting himself into the question.

'Why not use a bell?'

'The Christians have bells.'

'A drum?'

'There's too much blood in a drum.'

'A horn, like the Jews? That's a strong note.'

'There's too much of the animal left in a horn.'

'A trumpet.'

We fell silent. A flag, a drum, a ram's horn, a trumpet. Nobody was satisfied. A bell jangles the ear, a trumpet splits the head, a drum thumps up the blood and a flag goes too far in the other direction – it would never wake a sleeper.

Then I saw Abdullah Bin Zaid, one the the Helpers, coming forward shyly, inch by inch, so bashful that he seemed frightened of stirring the air – he who the next minute was going to stir the world. I saw at once that he had something to say, so I gave him my space near Muhammad.

'I had a dream, Messenger of God,' he began, 'and in this dream I heard the human voice calling us to prayer ...' He tailed off as if he thought no one was listening. 'An ordinary human voice.'

I looked quietly at Muhammad and saw that tears had come into his eyes. He leaned toward Abdullah. 'Yes, it will be so. Your dream was from God. It will be as you say ... the human voice.' He spoke so gently that I knew his word was the last word.

It was settled. But what voice, whose, how spoken? A soft voice, a sweet voice, a bellowing voice? My mind was racing in the possibilities of voices, a child's, a woman's, an old man's, a soldier's, a singer's, a scholar's, when I felt and I saw, the Prophet's hand on my shoulder.

'Your voice, Bilal.'

I did not at first take in what he said. When I felt his hand on my shoulder I jumped up without knowing why. My old instincts as a slave, which are hard to lose, had taught me to start moving even before understanding. I saw every face in the Mosque turned to me and then it dawned. But I who was to become the voice of Islam had nothing to say.

Saeed reached up and put his hand into mine and said something that still makes me cringe with pride. 'I wish I had such a gift to give to Islam.' Forgive me for repeating a compliment to myself; I say it because Saeed, whom I loved and who gave so much, said it.

Then Muhammad stood up and looked me in the face as only he could look at a man. But I have to admit that he said less than Saeed.

'You have the best voice, Bilal. Use it.'

'Messenger of God, what will I say?'

'Praise God, declare His Messenger, exhort to prayer, praise God. That is all. And all is enough.'

When the crown of his life is thrust upon a man, he does not always want it.

Even Muhammad himself when he received his call hid under blankets. I don't compare myself, only to say that I, too, wanted blankets. But there were none, no place to hide, no avoidance.

'Go up now and call them from up there,' the Prophet said.

I looked up to where he was sending me, a mud roof nearby.

You have all seen your minarets ... how graceful they stand, how secure the balconies, how good their elevation. A muezzin can catch his breath in the climb and the first glint of the horizon looking for the difference between a white thread and a black thread announcing the time of a new day. But when I climbed to make the first call I had to go up as best I could, pulling myself up, hand, belly, knees and foot. And even then, I was still below the palm trees. But worse was when I got up on that roof, I had nothing in my head. I had no-one to consult and no words, either to remember or forget.

Yet below me the upturned faces.

God knows that I, Bilal, the first muezzin can tell you about faces and how looking up at you, they lift you. The climbs were often dizzying but the faces would never let you fall.

That first time, with not one word to say, I looked back. Muhammad was near the third pillar, with Abu Bakr and Omar standing beside him. Omar was so tall that he seemed to be halfway up the tree. The Prophet raised his hands towards me in a lifting gesture, both encouraging me and telling me to begin.

'Praise God, declare His Messenger, exhort to prayer, praise God,' he had said. That was to be the order.

I turned away and thought. Then I threw back my head into the depth of my voice.

> God is most great. God is most great.
> I witness that there is no God but God.
> I witness that Muhammad is the Messenger of God.
> Come to prayer
> Come to good work.
> God is most great. God is most great.

Every day now, five times a day, through all Islam you hear these words. Yet I who first spoke them do not know where I found them. The Prophet had given me the order certainly, and when you have the shape you are more than halfway to the words. Yet still they must be thought. Did he when he gestured with his open hands give me the words? For I'll never believe I made them up myself. I believe the words were cast into me.

'*Allahu Akbar.* God is most great.'

When I came down Muhammad brought me to sit nearest him. The people flowed around us; a bunch of children came to giggle and run away. We made a fine pair, the Prophet of God sitting with the son of a slave. For a long time he said nothing and I admit that I, too, was lost in a mystery of my own. Then he had to go to lead the prayers. He rose and took me in his arms. 'Bilal, you have completed my Mosque,' was what he said. Thereupon, in the company of all those people who had come into the Mosque in answer to my call, I prostrated myself before God.

I, Bilal, had achieved my life.

(Taken from *Bilal*, by H. A. L. Craig, published by Quartet Books in 1977)

4 A THEMATIC APPROACH: SYMBOLS

Religion deals with complex concepts. Though some elements which we cover in RE with younger pupils can be described, observed and talked about in factual, concrete terms, the underlying beliefs, philosophies and concepts are essentially abstract. Moreover, these abstract concepts often relate to areas where there are no direct parallels in terms of human experience, so that people have to explain and describe them by means of analogy, metaphor, symbol, etc.

Most religions employ a combination of symbolic actions, symbolic words, symbolic food, symbolic dress, symbolic language and story, and symbolic objects, i.e. artefacts. Thus to understand religion it is necessary first to grasp what symbolism is. It is essential that pupils learn to look beyond a symbolic object, action or story to its underlying meaning.

Many primary schools already do work on signs and symbols, although this may be applied only to the six symbols commonly used to represent the main world faiths studied. The importance of this groundwork should not be underestimated, just because it may be commonplace. If something is valuable and it works, why discard it? The following introductory activity will not be new to all teachers but the development suggestions and rationale may provide an approach they have not considered before.

EXAMPLE: Unit of Work on Symbols

AIM: To introduce the concept of symbolism in religion and to explore its use in specific ways.

Introductory Activity

As a preliminary to understanding what symbolism is about, it is helpful for pupils to discover the difference between signs and symbols. Of course teachers will quickly realize that the distinction offered here is far more blurred in practice than I seem to be suggesting. In fact we often use the terms 'sign' and 'symbol' interchangeably. Nevertheless, symbols and symbolism are a vital element in any religion, as they attempt to express the inexpressible. Children need to be introduced to religious symbolism at an early stage if they are going to be able to grasp this fundamental aspect of religion. At first their knowledge and understanding will inevitably be partial, but as the subject is revisited over their school careers, it will hopefully deepen and enlarge.

A possible approach is to give pupils a number of common signs (e.g. road, disabled-toilet or telephone signs) and symbols (e.g. dove of peace, red poppy) and ask them to classify them as signs or symbols. The results of this can then be discussed by the class as a whole and a consensus arrived at. Some items may fall into both categories, but this does not matter, as it may help to illustrate and clarify the principles which are being applied in deciding which they are. It is this discussion which brings about an understanding of what a symbol is. From the final classification it should be possible for the pupils to suggest some guiding principles for determining whether something is a sign or a symbol and thence to come up with some sort of definition. This might be along the lines:

a **sign** gives information, is usually in picture form, and is easy to understand;

a **symbol** is also often in picture or diagrammatic form but represents a complex set of ideas.

I often use the idea of a secret code in explaining what a symbol is. One has to understand the code to be able to work out what the symbol stands for.

Younger children who may not be familiar with the term 'symbol' could be asked to pick out the signs and put them in one column then make a second column for the items left out. This could lead to a discussion of what the signs have in common, which could then be compared with the characteristics of the second list. It will be necessary for the teacher to give a greater input here, but even young children may at least be aware of the dove in the Noah's Ark story and the Armistice poppy, even if they do not yet know their full significance.

It must be stressed that the main point of this activity is to introduce the concept of symbols and symbolism. To reinforce the point, a good activity is for each child to design a symbol to represent him- or herself. This could be in the form of a badge or family crest. If time allows, a fun follow-up is to see if the children can identify each other's badges.

Introducing Religious Symbols

Most of the chapters in this book look at specific ways of using artefacts one or at most two at a time. Here, however, the method employs a number of items from the whole range of religions studied. Where a school's local Agreed Syllabus or 5–14 Document recommends looking at only two or three faiths at a particular key stage, teachers may prefer to choose artefacts from these religions only, depending on how the follow-up work is to be organized.

The artefacts here should be selected not so much for what they are as for the symbolism which they draw on. In some cases the symbolic value will lie in the artefact itself, e.g. a murti (statue) of a Hindu deity, while in others it may come from the symbols with which the object is decorated, e.g. a Hindu wedding garland decorated with the Aum (Om) symbol.

NOTE: Many of the artefacts in this activity are likely to be quite small and some could also be attractive, especially if they are in the form of jewellery. Items should be checked out to each group and counted back in again to avoid any 'losses'.

Introducing a Range of Religious Symbols

Resources	• Range of artefacts which are either symbols themselves or contain symbolism, e.g. Buddhist eight-spoked wheel, cross, paschal (Easter) candle decorated with alpha/omega, Aum symbol, diva lamp, menorah, flag of Pakistan (with star and crescent), Sikh flag (Nishan Sahib), symbolic jewellery • Paper and pencils • Teacher-prepared worksheets and resource sheets • Books for reference

Pupil Response	Activity
Cooperating Participating	Divide the children into small groups – four is an ideal size – and give each group a selection of artefacts.
Observing Discussing Deductive reasoning	Ask the children to look for religious symbols and to discuss which religion each symbol belongs to and why they have come to that conclusion. If some of the symbols are new to them, an introductory exercise may be needed before the artefacts are handed out.
Researching	Next ask the children to find out anything they can about the symbols. For younger pupils this task could be set out in the form of a worksheet with prompts such as 'Where might you find something like this?' or 'What does this stand for?' etc.
Collating/organizing Reporting/ summarizing	This research is then collated and the results reported back to the whole class.

Follow-up Activities

• Pupils could make a chart of the main symbols for each major world religion or for the religions being studied at that key stage. (It will save time and confusion if pupils are given a ready-drawn grid to help them, unless measuring straight parallel lines is a mathematical skill which is being taught at the same time!)

• Teachers might decide to leave room on the chart to add other information, such as names of major festivals, sacred writings, places of worship, etc., as the class reaches it. A large wall version could also be on display to help the children.

• One Manchester teacher I knew used to wear a different symbol each day and the pupils had to spot what it was. I have tried a similar exercise, though wearing six or seven symbols at once because I didn't see my class every day. It certainly awakened interest and was an activity which the children enjoyed, but is not to be recommended if you don't like being examined too closely!

Developing the Theme

The next stage will largely depend on the syllabus and programmes of study being followed in your school. Here are a number of different ways in which a basic understanding of symbolism in religion could be developed.

1. General symbols which occur in two or more religions could be explored, e.g. light or water. For more information on investigating the symbolism of light, see Chapter 8. For water, a good-starting point is to brainstorm in groups all the things which we use water for. When the groups' lists are compared it is likely that two ideas will feature in them all: water is necessary for life (drinking and plant growth) and is used for cleansing. These provide links with Christian baptism, ritual washing before prayer, worship or other important or ritual events across all the other major religions.

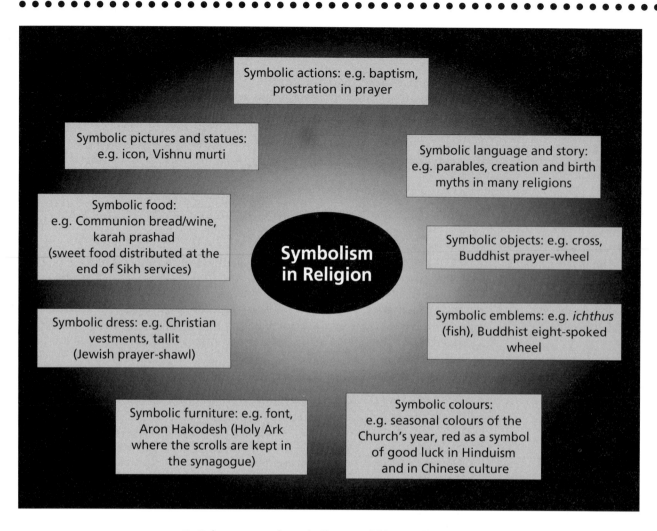

Symbolic actions: e.g. baptism, prostration in prayer

Symbolic pictures and statues: e.g. icon, Vishnu murti

Symbolic language and story: e.g. parables, creation and birth myths in many religions

Symbolic food: e.g. Communion bread/wine, karah prashad (sweet food distributed at the end of Sikh services)

Symbolism in Religion

Symbolic objects: e.g. cross, Buddhist prayer-wheel

Symbolic dress: e.g. Christian vestments, tallit (Jewish prayer-shawl)

Symbolic emblems: e.g. *ichthus* (fish), Buddhist eight-spoked wheel

Symbolic furniture: e.g. font, Aron Hakodesh (Holy Ark where the scrolls are kept in the synagogue)

Symbolic colours: e.g. seasonal colours of the Church's year, red as a symbol of good luck in Hinduism and in Chinese culture

2. Other types of symbolism could be explored. The diagram above indicates a range of possibilities. For each category I have included just two examples, one drawn from Christianity. Teachers should of course choose their own examples according to their own syllabus requirements.

3. Symbolism in places of worship could be explored through visits and/or using classroom resources such as videos and books.

4. The symbolism of particular artefacts could be explored.

EXAMPLE: Comparing Christian Crosses

AIM: To introduce Christian beliefs about the death, resurrection and ascension of Jesus.

The earliest Christian symbol was the fish, chosen because *ichthus*, the Greek word for 'fish', is an acronym for a sentence meaning 'Jesus Christ, God's Son, Saviour'. It is said that the cross was first adopted in the fourth century by the Emperor Constantine, who received a vision on the eve of a great battle in which he saw a cross and heard a voice saying, 'In this sign you shall conquer.'

In the following activity, the children compare three different types of cross:

- A crucifix, i.e. a cross with the body (corpus) of the dying Jesus on it.
- A plain or empty cross, i.e. with no body.
- A cross with the risen Jesus or Christ in Glory. Here the figure is fully clothed and upright with the palms of the hands open. The hands may still be nailed to the cross or the arms may be raised above the cross-bar and not attached. Christ in Glory will also be crowned.

Comparing Christian Crosses

Resources	
	• One set of three crosses – a crucifix, plain cross and cross with the risen Jesus or Christ in Glory – for each group. The crosses in different sets need not be identical designs.*
	• The questions could be in the form of worksheets for each group with space to write down or draw answers.

Pupil Response	Activity
Observing Describing Drawing Feeling Interpreting Empathizing	This is an activity for small groups of three or four. Lay out the three different types of cross in any order and set the children specific tasks, e.g. ask them to describe in detail and/or draw each cross. A group of three children could take it in turns to describe one cross to the rest of the group, who would then try to draw it (before seeing it for themselves, of course). An alternative to this is to ask the children their feelings about the cross as it is described to them, e.g. happy, sad, cruel.
Comparing Deducing Researching Sequencing Reasoning Discussing Cooperating	Continue with the questions: In what ways are the crosses the same? In what ways are they different? Do you think the differences matter? If so, which differences are important and why? Why do you think the crosses are different? What does each one mean? Can you put the crosses in order and relate them to particular times in the life of Jesus? Give reasons for your order and discuss it with the group. Why has the cross become the symbol of Christianity?
Discussing as class Listening	At this point the class should come together and discuss their findings. The teacher can then help them understand the sequence of events, how the different crosses highlight the death of Jesus (crucifix), the resurrection of Jesus from the dead (empty cross, symbolizing that Jesus has risen) and the risen Jesus (as he appeared on earth) or the ascended Jesus (Christ in Glory), and why these are so important to Christians.

* Where it is not possible to provide enough sets of crosses for each group, a compromise would be to have one set available at the front of the class. A child from each group could then examine one cross closely before describing it to the rest of his/her group. If the alternative activity is undertaken, the set of crosses could be supplemented in the groups by photographs or posters. At some point each group will need to see all three crosses together, however.

Follow-up Activities	
	• What can you find about other types of crosses, e.g. ankhs, Celtic crosses, Orthodox crosses? • Why do you think there are so many different types of crosses in Christianity? • Why do you think the cross is so important? • Why do people wear crosses as jewellery? • What do you think about people wearing an instrument of death as jewellery? • Should people who are not Christians wear crosses?

This example has been chosen to demonstrate the wealth of symbolism that can be drawn from a single artefact. Knowledge of this symbolism will help children to identify different murtis and, more important, will provide a simple introduction to the complex ideas which lie behind these representations of the Hindu deities.

Children could be shown several different portrayals of the god Vishnu, e.g. as a murti on his own, with Lakshmi (his wife) or in the Trimurti (i.e. with Brahma and Shiva). Here it may be necessary to supplement three-dimensional artefacts with pictures and photographs if it it not possible to get hold of enough different murtis. As with the crosses in the previous activity, the children could

The great god Vishnu
Some representations of Vishnu may not include all the symbols shown here. Instead the hands may be in different mudras (symbolic positions). These would typically be the abhaya mudra, with the upraised hand indicating blessing and reassurance, and the varada mudra, with the open palm pointing downwards to indicate a boon.

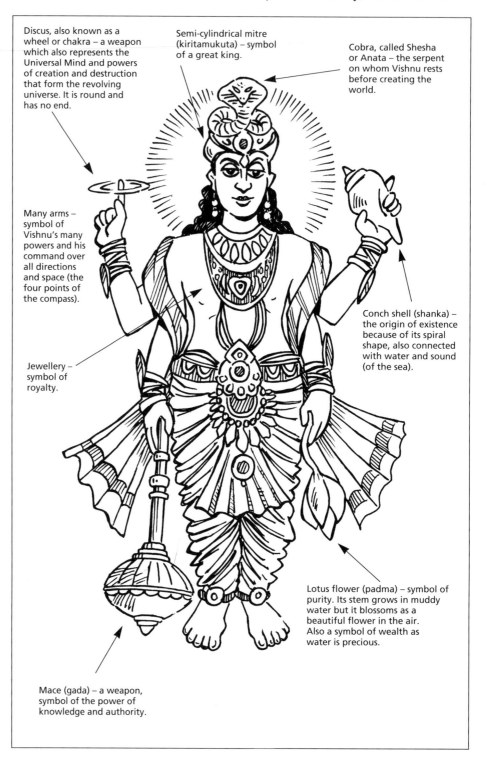

Discus, also known as a wheel or chakra – a weapon which also represents the Universal Mind and powers of creation and destruction that form the revolving universe. It is round and has no end.

Semi-cylindrical mitre (kiritamukuta) – symbol of a great king.

Cobra, called Shesha or Anata – the serpent on whom Vishnu rests before creating the world.

Many arms – symbol of Vishnu's many powers and his command over all directions and space (the four points of the compass).

Jewellery – symbol of royalty.

Conch shell (shanka) – the origin of existence because of its spiral shape, also connected with water and sound (of the sea).

Lotus flower (padma) – symbol of purity. Its stem grows in muddy water but it blossoms as a beautiful flower in the air. Also a symbol of wealth as water is precious.

Mace (gada) – a weapon, symbol of the power of knowledge and authority.

compare the various representations of Vishnu and answer the same first six questions listed. At this point the meanings of the common features/symbols could be discussed. It is likely that this will be the starting-point for further research, since the pupils themselves will probably be unable to provide the answers, though they may be able to suggest possible ideas which they can then confirm or reject.

An alternative approach would be to choose one murti per group and ask the children to list anything they can detect which might be symbolic. This might be an object which is being carried, a hand position, an item of clothing, and so on. Older and more-able children may be able to discuss what these things are and what they might mean before going on to find out about them. They could then draw or trace a picture of Vishnu and label each symbolic part. Alternatively, they could be provided with a drawing to label and explain.

Younger children could start with the artefacts plus a picture with the symbols indicated or with artefacts of the symbols. They could then be encouraged to talk about what the symbols might be, relating this to their own experience. For example, you could ask them where they would expect to find a conch shell and/or to describe it. From this they might make the connection that shells are found by the sea (water), they make a sound like the sea when you hold them to your ear, they have a spiral shape and they can be blown. The important point is to encourage the children to use their own reflective and intuitive responses to the symbols. When talking about symbols we should remember that each symbol can have diverse meanings and that those meanings can be coloured by an individual's experiences and responses to them. Moreover, meanings can change with time or with context, so the concept of a 'right' answer is redundant. The teacher's task is to relate the children's ideas to some of the traditional symbolic concepts which they represent. Many primary school books do not provide this type of information so the teacher may be advised to design a worksheet or information card to assist pupils in their research.

Another approach for younger children might be to draw each of the symbols on a separate piece of card. On three more sets of cards, write out the name of each symbol, a description of each symbol and its meaning. The children could match the descriptions to the names and meanings then transfer the information to a complete picture. It is suggested that this activity takes place in small groups, as the quality of the discussions which will have to take place in order to achieve the task is important. Constant monitoring and suggestions from the teacher will also help develop ideas and understanding of the symbolism.

Some of the concepts in Hinduism are quite hard to grasp, especially for younger children. For this reason, the teacher may decide to be more selective and choose only those symbols which it is felt the children can cope with at this point of their development. It is always possible to pick up a subject again at a more appropriate stage in their understanding. The aim of these activities is not *knowledge* about all the symbolic attributes of the god Vishnu. It is rather to build *understanding* of the importance of symbolism in religion and how it is used.

Resources on Symbols

Christian Festivals. Teacher's Book, by Jon Mayled, Living Festivals Series (RMEP). This contains a useful resource sheet on Christian symbols.

Signs and Symbols, by Olivia Bennet, Exploring Religion Series. This is out of print but good if you can borrow a copy.

Lord Vishnu's Revenge

This story is an example of another form of symbolism which is found through-out religious tradition: that of myth. A myth is essentially a story which is told to illustrate a truth or concept. The story itself may or may not be true, and believers from a religion to which a particular story belongs may disagree amongst themselves as to its literal truth. The importance of mythology, however, lies in the underlying concepts which the story is illustrating. In this example we are shown the Hindu belief in the omnipresence of Lord Vishnu, and how he will come to help his devotees in time of trouble and to strike out evil on the earth.

Lord Vishnu is one of the three great male deities of Hinduism: Brahma, the Creator, Vishnu, the Preserver, and Shiva, the Creator and Destroyer, or Regenerator, together known as the Trimurti. Hindus believe that in times of trouble Lord Vishnu has taken the form of an earthly creature and descended to earth to help conquer evil. These descents (or incarnations) are known as 'avatars'. Sometimes Vishnu took the form of an animal and sometimes he came as a man. The most famous of his avatars are Lord Rama, Lord Krishna and the Buddha. The last and tenth avatar, Kalki, is still to come.

This is a story of Lord Vishnu's fourth avatar, as the man-lion. It comes from the Puranas, a collection of Hindu religious writings containing many of the well-known stories about the deities.

Once there was a demon-king called Hiranyakashipu. He had been granted the great boon or favour by the gods that he could not be killed by man nor by beast nor by a weapon. Neither could he be killed inside nor outside a house, nor at night nor in the day, nor on earth nor in the sky. This, he believed, had made him invincible – no-one would ever be able to kill him.

Now, Hiranyakashipu had a son whom he named Prahlad. Prahlad was a good boy and he worshipped the great god Lord Vishnu. Day by day he would offer him worship and prayers. When his father heard of this, he flew into a mighty rage.

'How dare you worship anyone but me?' he cried. 'I am the greatest. I am invincible.' So he told his servants to take the boy and throw him down from the highest mountain peak.

Quick to obey their master's orders, the servants tied Prahlad up and hurled him down the steep mountainside, expecting to kill him. But Prahlad rolled softly down the mountain, rather like young children do when they're playing roly-poly down a grass slope. He arrived at the bottom without a scratch!

When Hiranyakashipu heard this he was even more angry.

'Throw him into the ocean and drown him,' he ordered. But the waves carried Prahlad gently back to shore and he was safe and dry once more.

The terrible demon-king tried deadly poison, he sent venomous snakes and a mad elephant to destroy his young son, but each time Prahlad emerged unharmed because Lord Vishnu protected him from the evil king and his wiles.

In desperation Hiranyakashipu commanded a great fire to be built. He ordered Prahlad's sister, the beautiful Holika, to take him into the fire with her. Now Holika too had been granted a boon. Hers was that fire would not hurt her, so she willingly picked up the young lad and set him on her knee in the midst of the flames.

The fire grew hotter and hotter as the flames roared upwards. It seemed impossible that anyone could withstand the heat of the blaze. Yet, when the flames died down, there amongst the glowing embers sat Prahlad, safe and unharmed. All that was left of his cruel sister Holika was a pile of grey ash at his feet.

Hiranyakashipu was at the end of his tether. He had tried everything he could think of to destroy Prahlad but nothing seemed to work. Finally he summoned the boy.

'Is this god whom you say you worship here now?' he demanded. Prahlad smiled.

'My Lord Vishnu is everywhere and in everything,' he answered. 'There is no place where he cannot be found.'

'Ah-ha,' sneered the wicked king craftily. 'If that is the case, let me see you embrace this pillar of red-hot iron, for your Lord Vishnu must surely be in there too.'

Without hesitation, Prahlad ran up to the pillar, threw his arms around it and hugged it tightly. Seeing that he was once again unharmed, Hiranyakashipu fell into a wild rage, and picking up his mace, he struck the pillar a mighty blow. Immediately the pillar shattered and there stood Lord Vishnu in the form of Narasimha. His body was strong and muscular, but his hair was a matted golden mane. His teeth were sharp and pointed and his hands had claws that could shred a man to pieces, for Narasimha was only half a human. His other half was a fearsome lion!

As twilight fell, Lord Vishnu as Narasimha pounced on the evil king on the threshold of his court. Crouching on his haunches he placed the king across his knees and tore him apart with his powerful claws. So Hiranyakashipu was killed – not by man or beast but by a half-man, half-lion, not by a weapon but by a lion's claws, not by day or by night but at twilight, not inside nor outside but on the threshold of his very own court, not on earth nor in the air but on the lap of the awesome Narasimha.

So it was that Prahlad's trust in the great Lord Vishnu, who is everywhere and who comes to the aid of those who believe in him, was rewarded, and he became king in place of Hiranyakashipu.

5 HOLY BOOKS

Although sacred writings consist of words, these texts take the physical form of three-dimensional, man-made objects and in this sense may be aptly described as religious artefacts. In sacred writings we have, *par excellence*, an example of the Divine communicating with humans, since for many believers their holy books contain the very words of the Divine Being. Not all believers take such a fundamental view of their scriptures, yet even the most liberal of interpretations acknowledge a Divine inspiration at work. These are books to be set aside from the humdrum activities of daily life and treated with reverence, because of what they contain – hence the terms 'holy' and 'sacred'.

The significance of sacred writings can be seen and appreciated from the way in which they have been preserved and how they are handled by believers. The rather careless attitude that is often displayed towards the Christian Bible is not typical of faiths in general nor of the Christian tradition as a whole. The handling of sacred writings needs to be approached with care.

Do's and Don'ts

All sacred writings should be treated with respect at all times. There are, however, some special points regarding the Qur'an, the Guru Granth Sahib and the Torah that teachers should be aware of in order to ensure that they are handled appropriately if brought into school.

The Guru Granth Sahib

This holy book is of supreme importance to Sikhs because the Tenth Guru, Gobind Singh, said that it would take the place of the human Gurus and provide Sikhs with all the guidance they required. So greatly is it venerated as a living teacher that it is treated as a special person. The name itself, Guru (teacher) Granth (collection) Sahib (a term of respect), indicates this. In Sikhism, the title 'Guru' is reserved for the ten human Gurus who founded the faith and the holy book.

In the gurdwara (Sikh temple), the Guru Granth Sahib has its own room. Each morning it is 'woken up', brought out in procession and placed upon a dais where it remains covered unless it is being read. Each night it is 'put to bed' again, i.e. returned to its room and covered for the night. Few Sikh families possess their own copy of the Guru Granth Sahib, as if it is kept in the home a special room has to be set aside for it, as an honoured guest. Here the ritual observed in the gurdwara will be carried out and it will be placed on a high shelf on its own, in a similar way to the Qur'an.

It is unlikely that many schools will possess a copy of the Guru Granth Sahib. I know of only one. This school was presented with a copy by their local gurdwara. It was fetched from the gurdwara in state: the path was strewn with flower petals, the book seated alone on the back seat of the car and transported to the school, where it was finally installed in a storeroom prepared solely for its use.

Smaller printed volumes containing part of the text, and sometimes a transliteration of the Gurmukhi script in which it is written, are available for use for study purposes instead of the actual Guru Granth Sahib.

The Torah

The Torah consists of the first five books of the Bible. Full-size, handwritten Torah scrolls (called Sefer Torah) are far too expensive and precious for use in schools, and there would be restrictions on the way they could be handled. Some of the most Orthodox Jews would say that only males could handle them. Certainly the parchment itself should never be touched, which is why a yad (pointer) is used when the scrolls are read.

For the classroom, smaller printed facsimiles are readily available and can be used by all, although the usual caveats about treating artefacts with respect apply. Similarly, authentic mezuzahs and tefillin are sacred objects because they contain passages from the Torah handwritten on parchment. Thus it may be more appropriate to use empty mezuzah cases and tefillin plus printed facsimiles of the texts in the classroom.

If the children are making 'Torah scrolls' themselves they should avoid using pictures, particularly of people, to decorate them. Texts from the Jewish Bible (not the New Testament!) are of course acceptable, as would be Hebrew writing, particularly the Shema or Ten Commandments.

Resist the temptation to open out scrolls fully, interesting though this may be. It is considered irreverent to do so. On a practical level it is totally inadvisable anyway. Before I knew that it was frowned upon (yes, we all make mistakes!), I unrolled the smallest-sized scroll in my classroom. It went right the way round the room and the chaos which resulted as we tried to wind it back up again had to be experienced to be believed.

The Qu'ran

For a Muslim, the Qur'an in its Arabic form contains the actual words which Allah gave to the Prophet Muhammad (Peace be upon him). The first revelation of the Qur'an to Muhammad (Pbuh), by the Angel Jibrael (Gabriel), occurred in 610 C.E. on Laylat-ul-Qadr (the Night of Power), the twenty-seventh day of Ramadan (the Muslim month of fasting), and the revelations continued until he died in 632 C.E. The verses were revealed in Arabic a few at a time and collected into 114 surahs (chapters). During Ramadan, Muslims may try to read the whole of the Qur'an, dividing it into thirty parts.

The words of the Qur'an have been passed down through the generations unaltered and unalterable. Because Muslims believe the Qur'an contains the very words of Allah given in Arabic, no word of it may be changed and it is always recited in Arabic during worship, as no translation could convey the exact meaning of every word. This is why Muslim children attend madrassa (Qur'anic school) in order to learn Arabic and to recite the Qur'an from memory.

Children begin to learn the Qur'an when they are between four and seven years old. Some Muslims have a party when a child recites the first passage he or she has learnt. Others have a celebration when a child has read the Qur'an through for the first time. The tradition of reciting the Qur'an goes back to the time of the Prophet Muhammad (Pbuh), who taught his followers by asking them to repeat the words after him.

Traditions in the treatment of the Qur'an vary but it will always be kept in a case or wrapped in a cloth, nothing will be placed on top of it and it will be stored off the ground/floor. Only calligraphy or pictures of mosques and/or Makkah will be hung above it. Hands are washed before it is read, women cover their heads and Muslims sometimes remove their shoes as a mark of respect (always if they are in the mosque). Sometimes the book is raised three times to the forehead and lips, symbolizing the desire to learn from it and showing love. Menstruating women should not touch the Qur'an as they are considered to be ritually unclean.

The Qur'an is placed on a stand (ra'el) when it is being read, so that it is always off the ground. It should be closed, and preferably covered, when not being read. Qur'an stands are generally made of wood. Some have beautiful inlaid patterns, some are carved in arabesque patterns, others are made of two pieces of plain wood. A ra'el is a book-stand and there is nothing 'special' about it in itself. Those commonly available in the U.K. are usually made in India, carved from a single piece of shesham wood, which is a renewable wood.

Translations of the Qur'an are allowed for study and are usually referred to as 'The Glorious Qur'an', 'The Qur'an Interpreted', etc., rather than just 'The Qur'an'. The Qur'an is easy to purchase in either its Arabic form or in Arabic/English or English-only versions, but note must be taken of the above points if a copy is bought for school use.

In schools, the Qur'an should be stored as described above, i.e. (i) wrapped in a cloth or in its slip-case, (ii) off the ground and/or on the highest shelf of a bookcase, (iii) with nothing on top of it. This holy book should be treated with respect at all times and hands should be washed before handling it. When it has been unwrapped, it should be placed on a stand and closed and covered when not in use.

Some teachers may feel it is appropriate to lift the Qur'an to the lips and and kiss it before opening it, as many Muslims do. However, this should be done only if the person feels sufficient respect and empathy with this action. Otherwise it becomes a mockery and is counterproductive. Always ask yourself, 'Is this appropriate for me to do, for my pupils to take part in?'

EXAMPLE: A Family Bible

AIM: To help children understand the special importance of the Bible for Christians.

This activity is based around a Family Bible. If one is not available, any other large 'lectern' Bible would suffice. The whole activity would be enhanced if a suitable lectern or book-stand was also available.

If the Bible was introduced as part of a church visit then the lectern or pulpit area would provide a useful focus. If the lectern was in the form of an eagle surmounting a globe, there would be additional symbolism and point to the exercise. The first two sections of the activity could be done beforehand in the classroom and linked to the church Bible with words like: 'You remember we discussed your favourite books in school ...'.

Investigating a Family Bible

Resources	• Large old Bible (a Victorian Family Bible would be ideal) • Lectern, if possible • Videos, posters, photographs from a variety of sources showing different Bibles in use • Flipchart/chalkboard • Differentiated worksheets • Books, etc., for pupil research

Pupil Response	Activity
Pair work Describing Empathizing Listening	Encourage pupils to talk in pairs about a favourite or special book or story. For example, why is it a favourite? Is it treated in a different way because of this?
Reporting accurately Listening	Ask each child to report back to the group what their 'pair partner' said. The best way to manage this will depend on the size of the class and the time available.
Observing Respect	Bring in or show pupils the Bible. Ideally this should be an old Bible, leather bound and heavy. For added effect, place it on a lectern. This section can be done in silence, without introduction or comment.
	Follow this with sections of videos, posters or photographs of the Bible in use, e.g. being kissed by the priest in an Orthodox church, being read by a woman (possibly a female priest/minister in an Anglican/Non-conformist church), being carried in procession in a Roman Catholic church, being read at home or in a church study group (Bible-reading notes for different age groups could be made available too). Examples of old Bibles, including illuminated manuscripts, could also be shown.
Questioning Brainstorming	Invite each child to think of a question about the big Bible or what they have just seen. The only requirement is that the pupil asking the question genuinely does not know the answer and is sensible and respectful. Write up the questions, preferably on a flipchart, but a chalkboard would suffice.
Researching Problem-solving	In the rest of the lesson or series of lessons, these questions, along with questions set by the teacher, form the basis of class research into the Bible, its origins and its importance in Christianity. Some pupils' questions may need to be put into an accessible form by the teacher. It does not matter if the teacher cannot answer them all: some questions have no answers!

Follow-up Activities	Pupils could: • Do some research into how the Bible came to be written in English. • Find out about the Welsh girl Mary Jones (see pages 38–39), the founding of the Bible Society and its work. • Try comparing a few verses from the Authorized or King James Version of the Bible with the translation in a modern edition, e.g. the Good News Bible or New International Version.

- Do some research into illuminated Gospels, e.g. those at Lindisfarne or the Book of Kells.
- Try painting some illuminated letters or practise some calligraphy.
- Make a collection or display of holy books. This could consist of a range of Bibles (e.g. a Hebrew Old Testament, a Greek New Testament, various English versions) or sacred texts from a number of religions. Teachers will need to think carefully about how the books can be handled and arranged in a safe and respectful way, particularly if more than one faith is involved.

If the Bible used in the activity is a Family Bible and belongs to a parent, for example, he or she could be invited to talk to the class about its history, if appropriate.

Other Ideas for Using Holy Books

- A similar activity can be accomplished with the Qur'an. In this case, bring the holy book into the classroom covered and on its stand. Before handling it, wash your hands. (Quickies or other wet-wipes can be used if water is not available in the classroom.) This is a particularly graphic introduction to the idea of the sacred (that which is set aside) and is far more memorable than simply telling pupils that Muslims wash before handling the Qur'an.

  As follow-up work, pupils could find out about and try practising some Arabic calligraphy or make a Qur'an cover or stand. Links could also be made with Laylat-ul-Qadr (Night of Power) in Ramadan (see page 33).

- Since full-size Torah scrolls are not available for classroom use (see above), teachers could either arrange a visit to a synagogue, where the scrolls could be seen *in situ*, and/or use videos showing, for example, the scrolls in procession or at a Bar Mitzvah or at Simchat Torah (a Jewish festival which celebrates finishing the complete annual reading of the Torah and beginning to read it again).

  As follow-up work, pupils could make Torah scrolls and decorate the mantle (cover) or try writing some Hebrew (remembering that this writing goes from right to left) or find out about the festivals of Simchat Torah and Shavuot (which celebrates the giving of the Law to Moses).

- Looking at the Guru Granth Sahib would likewise probably require a visit to a gurdwara or the use of videos showing it being installed in the morning or being 'put to bed' at night or being read at a special ceremony.

Resources on Holy Books

Discovering Sacred Texts Series (Heinemann). Consists of six titles on the major world faiths for lower secondary pupils, but also useful for teacher reference.

Succot and Simchat Torah, by Lynne Scholefield, Living Festivals Series (RMEP). Written for secondary pupils, but also useful for teacher reference.

Christianity Topic Book 2, by Margaret Cooling (RMEP). This activity book for primary schools includes the Bible as one of its four topics.

The Story of a Torah Scroll, by Eric Ray (Torah Aura Productions, ISBN 0 933873 04 2).

Address:
The Bible Society, Stonehill Green, Westlea, Swindon SN5 7DG

STORY

A Very Special Book

Katie came skipping out of the school gate. The bell had gone for home time and she looked for her mum amongst the group of mothers and fathers waiting at the gate. Where was she? Katie's forehead wrinkled in a slight frown but then she smiled. Grandma was there waving. Quickly she ran over to her gran and caught hold of her hand.

'Hello, Gran. Why are you here?' she asked. Grandma bent down and gave her a hug.

'Mummy's gone into hospital to have the baby,' she said. 'You know. So I'm looking after you instead.'

'Ooh, good,' said Katie. 'Can we make some scones for tea?' Grandma laughed.

'I should think so.' Together they walked off hand in hand and got into the car. Grandpa was there waiting.

'Hello, Katie. Had a good day?' he asked.

'Yes, thank you, Grandpa. We're going to make some scones for tea.'

'I hope I can have some jam with mine,' Grandpa chuckled.

Back at her grandparents' house, Katie helped make tea. Together they made scones. Katie's job was to roll them out and cut them with a special cutter shape that Grandma kept specially for her. Meanwhile Grandpa buttered and sliced bread that was so thin it was almost like paper. Only Grandpa could slice bread as thinly as that, Katie was sure.

They were just about to sit down for tea when the door-bell rang. Katie looked out of the window and saw her father's car. She ran quickly to the door and opened it.

'Hello, sweetheart,' he said, and picked Katie up and threw her in the air, laughing as he caught her again.

'Well?' said Grandma.

'Well?' said Grandpa as he appeared in the hall door.

'Well,' said Daddy, 'you've got a baby brother, Daniel, Katie.' Grandma and Grandpa clapped their hands in delight.

'Is everything all right?' they asked.

'Yes, fine,' replied Daddy and went on to say all sorts of boring things about weight and time.

'Can I see the baby, Daddy?' Katie asked, tugging at his sleeve. Daddy laughed again.

'In a little while,' he said, 'but first I have some phone calls to make and I can smell you've been baking. How about some of your – let me see – I bet they're scones.' Katie jumped up and down with excitement and pleasure and quickly went to get another plate, cup and saucer.

Later on that evening, after they had returned from the hospital, Katie was getting ready for bed. She put on her pyjamas and came downstairs for her bedtime drink. Grandma was in the best room.

'What are you doing, Grandma?' Katie asked. Grandma turned round.

'I'm getting out the Family Bible, so that we can add your new baby brother's name.' She lifted a big black book from the bookshelf. It looked very heavy. Katie watched as Grandma turned the pages. The writing was funny and big with odd squiggles here and there. She saw a few pictures too. The pages were beginning to turn yellow at the edges and the book looked very old.

'Is it worth much?' Katie asked.

'Well,' said Grandma, 'it all depends what you mean by "worth much". If you mean "Is it worth a lot of money?", I really don't know, though it is quite old. It's worth a lot to me, though, because it has all my family's names in it. Look!' She turned to the front page. There was a list of names, some of which Katie could hardy read because the ink was so faded. Grandma pointed down the list to the last name.

'There,' she said, 'that's you, Katie, and there's Daddy and there's your auntie Jean, and there's me.' Katie looked at the names.

'So,' continued Grandma, 'it is a very precious book. But it is also precious for another reason, and that is because of what is printed in it. Christians believe that God can speak to them through the Bible and it tells stories about Jesus, who they believe is God's very own Son. In the past, the Bible has been so precious that some people have died for the right to read it in their own language. Others, even in my lifetime, have become smugglers and risked imprisonment or death so that people could have a Bible of their own in countries where Bibles were forbidden. It's not just grown-ups for whom the Bible means so much. There was once a little girl, not much older than you, who went to an awful lot of trouble to get a Bible of her own. I know, you fetch your drink and get into bed and I'll tell you her story, if you like.'

As Katie snuggled down in bed Grandma began the story:

'Once there was a little girl called Mary Jones. She lived in Wales in a small village called Llanfihangel. Mary's mother and father were weavers but, though they worked hard, they never had much money. Mary did not go to school. In those days there weren't many schools, so Mary stayed at home and helped around the house, doing jobs like the washing, which all had to be done by hand in the local stream.

'On Sundays, she would put on her bonnet, wrap herself up in her woollen shawl and walk with her mother the two miles to chapel and back. Although she was only eight, Mary loved going to chapel. She liked singing the hymns but most of all she loved to hear the stories about Jesus which the minister read from the big chapel Bible. When she returned home she would repeat the stories to her father, who was not well enough to walk the distance to chapel. He would smile at her and say how well she could tell the stories from memory, but Mary always felt a little sad then. How she wished she could read the stories for herself. If only she could read ... if only she could have a Bible of her own ...

'It happened that Mrs Evans, a local farmer's wife, heard of Mary's wishes. She told Mary that if she ever learnt to read, she could go up to the farm and read the big Bible that was kept in the parlour there. Mary thanked her for her kindness, but how was she ever going to learn to read when there was no school and nobody to teach her?

'Two years passed, then one day there was great excitement in the Jones' house. Mary's father had been to the market to sell some cloth and had come back with the best news ever. There was going to be a school in the next village, Abergynolwyn, and Mary could go to it. She was so excited she simply couldn't wait.

'Eventually the great day came and Mary set off on the two-mile walk to school. She didn't mind the distance: she was going to learn to read, and she did. She studied hard, and before long she was helping other boys and girls in the school with their reading too. She remembered Mrs Evans' promise and every Saturday afternoon she would walk up to the farmhouse, spend an hour with the Bible then spend another hour walking back home again. She loved those Saturday afternoons but hated it when it was time to close the lovely book and put it back on the shelf for another week. "If only I had a Bible of my own," she thought. "Then I would have three times as much time to read the Bible 'cos I wouldn't have to walk there and back."

'That's how her great idea was born: she would buy a Bible of her own. But it wasn't going to be easy. She couldn't just pop into town on the bus and go to a bookshop to buy one. There weren't many books printed in Welsh, and Welsh was the language she spoke. There were even fewer bookshops, and her family was too poor to afford a Bible anyway.

'Mary was not put off, however. She decided to save up for her Bible. She did odd jobs: babysitting, laundry, chopping wood, feeding the neighbour's hens, anything at all. She didn't earn much: a farthing, a halfpenny, sometimes even a whole penny.'

A famous verse from
a Welsh Bible:

Canys felly y carodd
    Duw y byd,
    fal y rhoddodd efe
    eiunianedig Fab,
fel na chollen pwy
    bynnag a gredo
    yriddo ef,
ond caffael ohono
    fywyd tragwyddol.

(JOHN 3:16)

'An old penny, that is,' explained Grandma.

'One day kind Mrs Evans gave her a special present of two hens and a cockerel, so that Mary could sell the eggs they laid. Her savings grew but very slowly, and Mary was fifteen before she had enough money to buy her Bible.

'Now, where was she going to get it from? She went to see her local minister, who scratched his head and said that he thought the Reverend Mr Charles had Bibles but he lived in Bala. Bala? That was twenty-five miles [forty kilometres] away.'

Katie shrugged. 'Twenty-five miles? That's nothing. When we went on holiday last year Daddy drove us over two hundred miles there and another two hundred back,' she said. 'Easy peasy.'

Grandma shook her head. 'Not in those days. This was the year 1799. Motor cars hadn't been invented yet and there were no buses or trains either. A few rich people had horses or a pony-trap but everyone else had to walk. So that's what Mary did. She walked the full twenty-five miles to Bala, barefoot all the way because she didn't want to wear her shoes out – she didn't have enough money for another pair. It was a very long way, and Mary walked there all on her own. It was night time when she arrived and her feet were sore and blistered, but she didn't care. She was glad because soon she would have a Bible of her very own.

'First she had to find Pastor David Edwards, the man her own pastor (or minister) at home had told her to contact first. She stopped and asked someone the way and was soon standing on his doorstep. However, things didn't turn out as she had hoped.

'She knocked on the door and explained to Pastor Edwards why she was there. The pastor took her in and listened to her story. He was more than ready to take her to see the Reverend Mr Charles in the morning, meanwhile his wife found her a bed for the night.

'Next day Mary and Pastor Edwards arrived at Mr Charles' house. Mary told him the story of how she had learned to read so that she could read the Bible and how she had worked and saved for five years until she had enough money to buy one. Eagerly she held out her purse with all her savings, but Mr Charles shook his head sadly.

'"It's true. I do have some Bibles in Welsh but they are all spoken for. I'm afraid I don't have any left to sell to you." Imagine how Mary must have felt. She was bitterly disappointed. She had learned to read, saved up for all those years and walked twenty-five miles only to be told there wasn't a Bible for her.'

'What did she do?' Katie asked, aghast.

'She sat down and cried,' Grandma replied. 'She sobbed as though her heart would break. The Reverend Mr Charles was so touched by her story and so impressed by her courage and determination that he went to his bookshelf and took down one of the Bibles and gave it to her.

'"Someone else can wait for their Bible," he said. So it was a very happy young lady who set off home the next day with her precious Bible tucked under her arm.

'That's not quite the end of the story, though. Mr Charles now realized that Welsh people really needed to be able to read the Bible in their own language. He talked to Christian friends and was astonished by what they said.

'"If there is a need for Bibles in Welsh, there is a need for Bibles in every language. If for Wales, why not for the world?" they agreed. Together they set up a society they called the British and Foreign Bible Society. It's still going today but has changed its name to the Bible Society. It makes Bibles available in different languages for people all over the world, so that they can read it for themselves in the language they speak.'

Katie sighed sleepily. 'I'm glad Mary got her Bible in the end,' she said. 'Can I try to read your Bible tomorrow, Grandma?'

Grandma nodded, bent down to kiss her forehead and wrapped the covers round her tightly. 'Night night, little one. Sweet dreams,' she whispered ... but Katie was already fast asleep.

ARTEFACTS FOR DISPLAY

The best classrooms are those with plenty of visual stimulus in the form of both children's work and posters, models, displays and living things. Displays of religious artefacts can be very effective, but do need special attention if we are to put over the right messages and not offend members of the faith communities.

Some schools display their artefacts in a locked cabinet. There are good reasons for this. Apart from possible breakages and theft, some artefacts, such as the Sikh kirpan (sword), should not be handled without supervision. However, simply displaying a jumble of artefacts is not necessarily going to create an impact or be of great teaching value. It may also raise problems if artefacts from two or more religions are crowded together.

For maximum effect, displays should be changed at least every half term. A basically static display which is added to or altered slightly throughout that period creates even more interest. This technique can be used with great effect with a Nativity scene, for example. Here the Wise Men can change position daily as if journeying towards the manger, to arrive in time for Christmas or Epiphany (depending on how long the display is left up). Younger children, in particular, love to spot the new position each day when they enter the classroom.

Displays to which the children contribute ideas, work or artefacts from home have added value. It is, of course, important to ensure that artefacts on loan will come to no harm and are returned when the display is dismantled.

EXAMPLE: A Display on Buddhism

AIM: To develop some understanding of the reverence in which the Buddha is held by Buddhists as part of a course on the Buddha and his teaching.

ARTEFACTS REQUIRED:

- Buddha rupa (statue)
- Seven offering-bowls
- Incense sticks and holder
- Posters or thangkas of the Buddha or Bodhisattas
  (A thangka is a painting, usually on cloth, which can be used as an aid to meditation. A Bodhisatta is a being destined to achieve Enlightenment and become a Buddha.)
- Flowers
- Lamp, e.g. a butter-lamp
- Cloth

Display the statue on a small dais covered with the cloth: Buddha rupas should be placed at a higher level than surrounding items as a mark of respect. Posters and thangkas may be displayed on the wall or a screen behind the rupa and

Display on Buddhism

the seven offering-bowls positioned in a line or semicircle in front of the image. If a lamp and incense-holder are used the number of bowls could be reduced to five.

This arrangement is similar to the lay-out of a Buddhist shrine. The seven offering-bowls represent the gifts which would be offered to a respected guest: water for washing, water to drink, light, fragrance, flowers, music and food. At a shrine the bowls would be filled with water to symbolize these elements, though it is also common for Buddhists to offer actual incense, food, flowers and light as well.

Whether it is appropriate to go beyond the simple display and place 'offerings' before the rupa is a matter for individual judgement. Some teachers would feel happy with placing flowers before the rupa and even lighting the lamp and/or incense at some point during the day, perhaps during an act of collective worship or some other quiet time. Others would feel unhappy doing this as it might suggest a reverence for the Buddha which they would regard as compromising their own faith or that of their pupils. It should be noted, however, that such actions would not constitute 'worship' as this is a concept which Buddhists would not use.

Do's and Don'ts

Religious artefacts should, of course, be treated with respect when a display is being set up or dismantled, as well as when they are in place. If artefacts from more than one faith are on display, consideration should also be given to their relative positions. An example of this occurred locally when children's work was displayed in the cathedral. One school had been looking at Buddhism as the predominant religion of the area they were studying. They had constructed a magnificent golden image of the Buddha from papier mâché and set it up in the form of a shrine. However, the space originally allotted to them was in front of the Jesus chapel. This was felt to be somewhat inappropriate by the cathedral hierarchy but a compromise was easily reached by re-siting the display down a nearby aisle.

There are no hard and fast rules which can be applied in these sorts of circumstances. Teachers can be guided only by common sense and sensitivity to the issues which might be raised. In general, if the usual ground rules of respect and care are applied and the advice on how to handle particular artefacts given elsewhere in this book is followed, there are unlikely to be any serious problems. It is probably best to avoid mixing religions unless the display is illustrating a theme such as 'Prayer' or 'Festivals of Light' or is supporting independent work by pupils on different topics. Even then it is less confusing to group artefacts from the same religion together.

Some artefacts are designed for permanent display *in their religious setting.* Obvious examples of these would be the cross or crucifix in Christianity, the mezuzah in Judaism or the Sikh flag which flies outside every gurdwara. There is an obvious difference between contexts like this and the secular classroom, however.

In a Roman Catholic or Church of England school it may be a natural, even expected, part of the school ethos to have a cross, crucifix or statue of Mary (depending on the tradition) in the hall, entrance or in each classroom. This is a focus and a statement of the foundation faith of the school. In other words, it is being displayed as an aid to worship and has a religious and ritual context. The same could be said of a mezuzah in a Jewish school.

Before making any artefact a permanent or even semi-permanent fixture in a classroom we need to ask ourselves what message it is giving and whether this is what we want to convey to the children, parents and visitors to the school. Another consideration must be how it would be viewed by members of the faith community. Many would not be happy with a ritual object being on permanent display in a classroom where it will be difficult to treat it with proper respect at all times.

Thus, for example, we could ask if it is appropriate to put a mezuzah on the doorpost of a *secular* classroom. A mezuzah with an authentic mezuzah scroll containing the Shema handwritten on parchment inside it is a ritual artefact and raises questions about how pupils might/should react to it and treat it. It is likely that many Jews would be unhappy about its presence in a classroom in this way. It would be wrong to expect non-Jewish children to treat it as a Jew would, but if they do not, there seems little purpose in placing it on the doorpost. I doubt whether it would make any difference if the scroll was removed since its absence would not be apparent from the outside. The crunch question is: 'What is the purpose of placing a mezuzah on a classroom doorpost?' I suspect the answer is often 'novelty value', in which case it should be rejected. The same argument, however, would not necessarily hold good in the home corner. If the purpose here is to teach young children what you would find in a Jewish home, then the mezuzah case (without the scroll) has to be there.

There is no simple answer here. It is sometimes easier if the question is given a more familiar context, e.g. 'What would you think if you walked into a classroom and saw a cross or crucifix in the middle of the wall on permanent "display"?' Most people would pick up the message 'This is a Christian classroom', i.e. it gives the artefact a ritual context. The same message may be given by a mezuzah fixed to the doorpost in a secular classroom. In cases of doubt it may help to turn the argument around and ask, 'Would it be appropriate to place a cross in a classroom of a Jewish school?' At the end of the day, the pertinent questions have to be: 'What is the purpose of displaying this particular artefact in this way?' and 'Will it offend anyone if it is displayed like this?'

Other Ideas for Displays

- Use of shapes can enliven displays. For example, children's work (pictures, poems, etc.) on the Easter theme 'New Life' could be arranged in the form of a large cross. An Easter garden, paschal candle and other Easter symbols could be placed at the base of the cross. The whole display could be set up at the entrance of the room where collective acts of worship are held in the period leading up to Easter, or used as a focal point for an act of worship itself. Additional benefit can be gained from this if the display spans the Easter break, so that the bleakness of the sealed tomb contrasts with the living flowers and empty tomb of the post-Resurrection garden.

- If work has been done on the Jewish festival of Pesach (Passover), it would be appropriate to set a Seder table, perhaps with a backdrop of the Ten Plagues in the form of children's work. An attractive illustrated Hagadah could be left open on the table and a new page turned each day to reveal the next part of the story.

Resources on Displays

Looking into Religion: Religious Education and Works of Art, by Dennis Starkings. Article in *RESOURCE*, vol. 13, no. 2 (Spring 1991).

STORY

The Garden Buddha

It was Saturday and the twins were full of excitement. They were going to their dad's for the week-end and visiting his new home for the first time. A short beep on the horn told them he had arrived, and quickly they slipped their rucksacks onto their backs and ran down the drive.

'Hi, kids,' their dad greeted them, throwing their bags into the boot of the car and hugging them both together. 'Into the car with you. We've got lots to do today, so don't hang about. Kelly, you can sit in the front going and swap over with Ben after we've been to the Garden Centre,' he commanded, before they could start an argument. The car drove off and the twins turned to wave to their mother, who was standing in the doorway to see them off.

The first stop was the Garden Centre because Dad wanted to buy some shrubs for his new garden. 'Now don't go causing trouble, you two,' he shouted after them as he headed for the rose bushes. 'We'll meet back here in half an hour. I might even treat you to an ice-cream – if you're good. Oh, and make sure you keep together. I don't want you getting lost,' he added.

Kelly and Ben wandered around the indoor displays for a few minutes but it wasn't very interesting.

'Let's go outside,' suggested Ben. 'I think I saw an adventure park there.' They ran through the automatic doors out into the bright sunshine. Suddenly Kelly stopped.

'Look at that,' she pointed. In front of her was the garden-ornament department. There were rows of gnomes with brightly painted hats in various poses. There were stone squirrels, foxes and badgers, and there were stone Buddhas sitting deep in meditation.

'What about it?' complained Ben, who was far more interested in trying out the assault course on the playground.

'Well,' mused Kelly, 'don't you think it's a bit odd putting Buddhas in a garden? I mean, we were talking about him in class last week. Remember how Mrs Marsh told us what a holy man he was and how his followers became part of a religion called Buddhism?'

Ben nodded. 'Yes, but so what?'

'Well,' continued Kelly thoughtfully, 'who would want one of those statues? Are there lots of Buddhist people who buy them or do other people put them in their gardens along with those funny gnomes?'

Ben shrugged. 'Well, the video we watched showed those monks putting up a big statue of the Buddha in their garden, so I suppose it's all right.'

'Yes,' agreed Kelly, 'but it's hardly the same as us having one in the garden. Wouldn't it be – I can't remember the word Mrs Marsh used – sort of not nice to treat such a special religious figure in the same way as those garden gnomes. Look, that one's showing his bottom!'

'Mmm,' Ben wrinkled up his nose. 'I think the word was "disrespectful". I suppose it might be a bit like putting one of those crosses with a Jesus on it in the garden. Oh, I don't know. C'mon, Sis. I'll beat you to the swings.' With that they raced off down the path.

An ice-cream later they were at the next stop: the lighting department of a DIY store.

'I won't be a minute,' Dad said. 'I've just got to pick up a new lampshade for the lounge. Don't touch anything,' he called over his shoulder. Off he went, the twins trailing behind among the shelves of lamps. Suddenly Ben tugged at Kelly's arm.

'Get off,' she snapped. She was beginning to feel tired and bored.

'Please yourself,' Ben shrugged. 'I only wanted to show you something. I thought you might be interested, but it's your loss not mine,' he responded in an airy fashion.

That of course made things different. Kelly was full of curiosity. She nudged her brother: 'Go on, tell.'

Ben pointed. 'Look at that Buddha.' Kelly turned and stared. In front of her was a beautiful white Buddha, decorated with flecks of gold. He was sitting cross-legged, in the lotus position, his face was calm and peaceful, and the fingers of his right hand pointed downward to the ground in what Kelly recognized as the 'earth touching' position. Yet for Kelly it was totally spoiled by the bulb and lampshade 'growing' from the Buddha's head.

Kelly looked at Ben and both twins shook their head. 'That can't be right,' they agreed. 'Let's ask Dad.' Their father, however, was far too busy trying to choose between a clear glass or pale green shade and said that he really had no idea, and why didn't they ask Mrs Marsh at school on Monday.

On Mondays, after registration and morning assembly, Mrs Marsh always gave them a few minutes to tell the class any news. Ben and Kelly told their news together, each interrupting the other if their twin had left something out. It was Ben who brought up the subject of the Buddhas. Mrs Marsh listened with interest.

'That's very observant of you both,' she nodded as they finished their account. 'Now, what do the rest of you think?' A few minutes of discussion followed. Some children thought that it didn't really matter what you did with the Buddhas. Others felt more like Ben and Kelly, that religious statues or rupas, as Mrs Marsh said the Buddha statues were called, should be treated with respect, even by people who weren't Buddhists themselves.

Then Kelly's best friend, Kim, put her hand up and asked, 'What would a real Buddhist feel about it?'

Mrs Marsh shook her head. 'To be honest, I don't know,' she said, 'but I have a friend who's a Buddhist. I'll ring him up and see what he says. We'll talk about this again later.'

'Later' turned out to be the next week, and Mrs Marsh didn't just report back to the class, she brought her Buddhist friend, Brian, to talk to them in person. The children explained their problem to him.

'Well,' he said, 'I have a statue of the Buddha in my garden.'

'Yes, but that's different,' interrupted Jamie. 'After all, you believe in it. What about people who don't?'

'I think that's probably all right too,' suggested Brian. 'You see, a Buddha rupa to me is a symbol of my aspiration. I mean, it's what I'm aiming for,' he added, as he saw the puzzled look on their faces. 'I too want to be like the Buddha, so when I see his image it reminds me of what I am aiming for. A garden is a nice peaceful setting for a Buddha. It's a place where you can relax and think. Non-Buddhists might also find such a statue in their garden helps them think about who they are and what is important to them. I don't think there's anything wrong with that.'

'But what about the gnomes?' objected Kelly. Brian nodded in agreement.

'I suppose that is different. I'd imagined a Buddha set in a beautiful garden, surrounded by grass and flowers and trees. I agree that if it is just one of a collection of "funny" ornaments it would be different. It looks as though what we are saying is that it depends on *why* a person has put the statue there and how he or she sees it. I certainly wouldn't be very happy if it were seen as an object of fun.'

'What about the Buddha lampstand?' asked another girl.

Brian shook his head. 'Now that's easy. A Buddha is a sacred image. It is a reminder of what we as Buddhists are aiming for. Its place is somewhere special, like a shrine. It certainly shouldn't be used as a functional object – something that does an ordinary job around the house, for example,' he explained.

The children asked lots more questions. Then Brian used the school Buddha from Mrs Marsh's collection of religious artefacts to show the children what the various parts of the rupa meant. He also demonstrated how to create a Buddhist shrine with the rupa seated in pride of place.

Afterwards the children each made a picture of a scene from the life of the Buddha and together the class wrote a short play about his life which they acted to the rest of the school one assembly. What do you think the centrepiece on the Head's table that morning was, surrounded by the children's pictures and a vase of flowers? You've guessed it: the Buddha rupa!

7 ARTEFACTS FOR DRAMA,
ROLE-PLAY AND DEMONSTRATION

There is no doubt that children learn best when they are actively involved in their own learning. Drama, role-play and demonstrations in which they can participate all afford this opportunity. These activities develop empathy and can lead to a deeper understanding of some of the difficult and abstract concepts with which religion grapples. They offer the opportunity for research and study, and encourage cooperation and team work amongst members of the class or group. In addition they involve many other skills – music, dance, art, creative writing – giving children who may not find it easy to contribute to more 'academic' lessons the opportunity to share with others. Above all, these activities can be fun, and the best learning takes place when the lesson is an enjoyable experience.

Do's and Don'ts

Additional realism and enjoyment can be achieved in drama, role-play and demonstrations if genuine clothes and props (i.e. artefacts) are used. However, some care does need to be taken over what is appropriate in this regard. It is impossible to give hard and fast rules as to what may or may not be done here: the final decision has to rest with the teacher in each case.

The main requirement is sensitivity and respect on the part of both staff and pupils. For example, Asian clothes are not religious but cultural and most Asian people would not object to children dressing up in them. However, the same is not true of the Sikh turban or of Buddhist monk's robes. These are not 'dressing-up' clothes which can be stuffed in a dressing-up box along with top hats, crinolines and wimples. They are articles which have a religious significance and should be treated as such. On the other hand, if pupils understand how and why these clothes are normally worn and treat them with respect, it may be acceptable to wear them, if doing so is an essential part of a drama or role-play and adds to their overall religious understanding. The test is:

- Are the clothes going to be treated properly and with respect in an educational way?
- Will they add to the pupils' understanding?
- Will wearing them give offence?

The sample unit below could incorporate an enactment of a Seder, the ritual meal at Pesach (Passover). This has become an increasingly popular activity over the past twenty years, but there are questions which need to be considered when planning demonstrations of this type. Essentially the actual ceremony is a *ritual act*. Therefore it is most important that the issues are thought through carefully if we are to avoid turning a primarily religious occasion into a mockery.

The Seder (literally, 'order') is a meal set in the home which is redolent of Jewish religion and history. It is more than a retelling of historical events. It involves reliving and participating in those events today: making real in the present the events of the past.

> In every generation it is a person's duty to consider himself *as if he personally had come forth from Egypt* [my italics], as it is said: 'On that day you shall tell your son, saying, it is because of what the Lord has done for me when I came forth out of Egypt.' (Exodus 13:8) For it was not our forefathers alone that the Holy One, Blessed be He, redeemed, *but us as well* [my italics].
>
> (From the Hagadah)

The Seder is also an act of worship since it contains blessings and prayers. Therefore we have to decide whether or not it is appropriate for non-Jews to lead a Seder in the same way as it is led in Jewish homes each Pesach and to ask our pupils to join in what could be regarded as an act of worship. A helpful analogy might be a teacher or member of the class conducting a Mass in the classroom.

There is, however, room for a compromise here. Where there is a local Jewish community it may be possible to invite someone to share with the children what happens at the Seder. The key word here is 'share'. The children would be shown what Pesach means to a Jew and they would be invited to watch and join in when they felt it was appropriate.

If there is no local Jewish community, the teacher or class members might take the pupils through the order. They could *demonstrate* what happens at each stage of the ritual, and give appropriate explanations of the actions and their meaning. However, the teacher and the pupils must remain 'removed' from the events. In other words, each stage should be introduced by saying something along the lines: 'At this point the head of the house washes his hands, like this,' then demonstrating the action. This results in a true demonstration and not a mimicking of a ritual act. Throughout, children and teacher should show due respect and the emphasis should remain on the *educational* aspect of the activity so that it does not become a mock Seder.

Another example of this distinction can be found in the Muslim prayer postures. As a teacher, I might indicate the various positions used in a unit of prayer (ra'kah) separately, but I would never, being a non-Muslim, perform a complete ra'kah, simultaneously reciting the prayers. Nor would I ask my pupils to do so. To demonstrate the postures is one thing, but to become involved in the ritual act of prayer is quite another.

In drama and role-play the children take on the character and role of the individuals being portrayed. In this case they are aware that it is an assumed role and the essence of the activity is an 'acting out'. However immersed in their role they appear to be at the time, once the drama has ended they can step back into real life. The empathy and feelings may still be retained but there is also the necessary distancing. This can be reinforced by careful debriefing by the teacher.

Religious stories such as parts of the Rama/Sita epic and parables are popular subjects for drama and lend themselves to it. Other religious historical events could also be acted out but teachers should note that any physical portrayal of the Prophet Muhammad (Peace be upon him) would give offence. A bit of ingenuity can get around the problem, e.g. giving Muhammad's words to a narrator. The very fact that the part of Muhammad (Pbuh) cannot be played by anyone is in itself a valuable teaching opportunity. Teachers might like to reflect that the first cinema portrayals of Jesus took the same stance, with only his voice being heard for reasons of reverence. Later this developed to include shots from the back but the face was not shown. Modern portrayals have no such reserve, as 'The Last Temptation of Christ' indicates. Again, some useful discussions can arise from this, particularly with older children.

EXAMPLE: Unit of Work on Pesach (Passover)

Aim: To explore some central themes of Judaism, in particular God's saving acts in history, especially in the redemption of his people from slavery in Egypt through the Exodus, and its continuing expression in modern Judaism.

This unit could culminate in some form of demonstration of the Seder.

Another word of warning is needed here. Pesach or Passover is an important Jewish festival with its own history, form and meaning. It exists quite apart from Christianity and it is important that teachers remember this and do not rob it of its Jewish significance. It is actually upsetting, even offensive, to the Jewish community if the Passover is taught in schools only in a 'Christian' context, i.e. to aid understanding of the Last Supper Jesus had with his disciples. It will also mislead the children who are being taught. Of course, this does not preclude references to Pesach when studying Christianity, as it is impossible to understand Christianity fully without some knowledge of the Judaism out of which it grew. It is rather a matter of emphasis and approach.

Preliminary Sessions

Before looking at the modern festival of Pesach, children need to be familiar with its biblical origins. The stories of the persecution of the Hebrews as slaves in Egypt, the birth of Moses, his flight to Midian, his call at the burning bush, his return to Egypt and the sending of the Ten Plagues should therefore be taught in some detail. This is a necessary preparation as many of these events are alluded to in the Hagadah (the book containing the order for the Seder) and Pesach will not make sense to the children without this background knowledge and context.

Investigating a Seder Plate

Aim: To stimulate enquiry about the design of a Seder plate and the purpose behind that design (i.e. its symbolism).

Investigating a Seder Plate

Resources	• One Seder plate per group • Worksheets plus as wide a range of relevant books and other resources as possible, e.g. videos, posters, Jewish visitor, Pesach artefacts, food, songs

Pupil Response	Activity
Observing Describing (oral skills)	Divide the children into small groups of four to six (depending on the resources available). Give each group a Seder plate and ask the children to describe it orally in the group. This is essentially to aid their observation of the design of the plate and to enable them to continue into the brainstorming exercise.
Brainstorming Questioning Summarizing Ranking Researching	Ask each group to brainstorm questions about their plate. These questions should then be collated by the group and could, with additional questions set by the teacher, form the basis for further research. Some of the pupils' questions may need to be put into an accessible form by the teacher. It does not matter if the teacher cannot answer them all without further consultation. See opposite for some lines of enquiry pupils could follow.
Using presentation skills, e.g. oral communication, cooperation, confidence-building, drawing, reading, prioritizing	Encourage each group to make a presentation on Pesach to the rest of the class. The children themselves, with teacher assistance where appropriate, should determine the content and format, e.g. they could produce a drama (historical or modern), a video, an audiotape, an explanation of what happens at a Seder, its significance and symbolism, or a demonstration.

- At what time of year does Pesach take place?
- Find out four other names for this festival.
- What preparations take place in the weeks leading up to the festival? Be as detailed as you can. Find out what a candle and feather are used for and what 'chametz' means.
- Give a brief explanation of what the festival is celebrating.
- Make a glossary (dictionary) of the special words you meet in this project.

- What is meant by 'kosher'?
- Find out about Jewish dietary laws. What foods may be eaten? Which foods may not? What should Jews never mix together? What does a Jewish kitchen look like? (You can put some of this information in the form of a diagram or chart.)
- Draw or make a Seder plate and label the foods on it.
- Describe the symbolic meaning of each of the foods.
- What is matzah?
- Find a recipe for charoseth.
- What does the word 'Seder' mean?

Ideas for Pupil Research on Pesach (Passover)

- In what book is the Pesach service found? What does the name of the book mean?
- Write out briefly the order of the Pesach service.
- What are the four questions which are asked? Who asks them?
- What do the four glasses of wine represent?
- Why is wine spilt during the service?
- Draw a diagram of the Ten Plagues.
- What is the significance of the fifth glass of wine and the open door?
- What is the afikomen and what game is played with it?
- Copy out the words of one of the songs sung at Pesach.

- Write out the prayer which celebrates Pesach as a festival of freedom.
- Why do you think freedom is such an important theme at Pesach?
- In what way is the plight of those who are not free remembered during the meal?
- Read the account of the celebration of Pesach in the Warsaw ghetto during the Second World War in the book *Mila 18*, by Leon Uris.
- Make a collage or poster of things which represent freedom to you.
- Write a poem on freedom.

Other Ideas for Drama, Role-play or Demonstrations

- Rites of passage, especially weddings, also some initiation ceremonies.
- Special events, e.g. an Eid (Id) party.

Remember that the real value for RE lies in the discussions and preparations which need to take place before the actual drama, role-play or demonstration is performed.

Resources on Pesach

The following extract by Rabbi John Rayner, from *Passover Hagadah* (Union of Liberal and Progressive Synagogues, London, 1981) expresses very clearly the sense of freedom which underlies the celebration of Pesach:

What they experienced, they remembered, and told their children, and they theirs.

From generation to generation, the story was retold, and we are here to tell it yet again.

We too give thanks for Israel's liberation; and we too remember what it means to be a slave.

And so we pray for all who are still fettered, all who are still denied their human rights.

Let all God's children sit at His table,
drink the wine of deliverance,
eat the bread of freedom:
freedom from bondage
and freedom from oppression,
freedom from hunger
and freedom from want,
freedom from hatred
and freedom from fear,
freedom to think
and freedom to speak,
freedom to learn
and freedom to love,
freedom to hope
and freedom to rejoice;
soon, in our days.
Amen

For those wishing to conduct a demonstration Seder themselves, the following books are recommended as they guide teachers through the main sections, and include notes on how to prepare for the demonstration:

Passover Seder for Primary Schools, compiled by A. Clark and S. Malyan (Wandsworth Borough Council Education Dept, Professional Centre, Franciscan Road, Tooting, London SW17 8HE).

The Seder Handbook, by Clive Lawton (Central Jewish Lecture and Information Centre).

The Passover Celebration: A Passover Hagadah, edited by Rabbi Leon Klenicki (Anti-Defamation League of B'nai B'rith and the Liturgy Training Program of the R.C. Archdiocese of Chicago, available from Articles of Faith Ltd).

The following would be found on a table laid for the Seder:

- Seder plate with appropriate foods: shank bone of lamb, roasted egg, bitter herbs, green vegetable (usually lettuce or parsley), charoseth (a mixture of apple, nuts and cinnamon), salt water
- Kiddush cup and (kosher) red wine
- Elijah's cup
- Matzot and (matzah) cover
- Pair of candles and candlesticks
- Hagadah

OTHER USEFUL BOOKS:

Children's Hagadah (Routledge and Kegan Paul, available from Articles of Faith Ltd).

Passover, by Lynne Scholefield, and *Jewish Festivals. Teacher's Book*, by Jon Mayled, Living Festivals Series (RMEP).

Mila 18, by Leon Uris (Corgi). Novel based on the events of the Warsaw uprising in April 1943. Not a pupil's book but provides a feel for the importance of the Seder and other Jewish rituals in time of persecution.

VIDEOS:

Pesach Video (ex-ILEA production with Clive Lawton).

The Animated Hagadah (Scorpus Films). Uses animated clay figures, a style not appreciated by everyone. There is also a book in the same vein.

MUSIC:

A Survivor from Warsaw. This cantata by Schoenburg is his memorial to the Jews of Warsaw.

Sharon Sings Seder Songs and *Songs for a Family Seder* (Wimbledon and District Synagogue, 44–46 Worple Road, London SW19 4EJ). These cassettes include songs in Hebrew and English versions.

STORY

The Different Night

The Warsaw ghetto was created in October 1940 and initially contained about half a million Jews. A Jew found outside this area could be summarily executed. Inside, conditions were terrible: overcrowding, disease and starvation killed many. In July 1942 the Nazis began to transport the population to the extermination camps: Chelmno, Treblinka, Auschwitz. In April 1943 the Jews remaining in Warsaw, estimated to number less than fourteen thousand, rose up against their oppressors. Without outside support, their resistance nevertheless lasted a month, before they were either dead or taken to the gas-chambers.

The rabbi's prayer 'Behold, ...' quoted in the story was in fact used in one of the concentration camps, Bergen Belsen, in 1944 at Pesach, when there were no mazot available. It is used here with poetic licence: the principle remains the same! The full prayer appears in *The Fourth World Hagadah*, compiled by J. Harris and J. Schuldenfrei (World Union of Jewish Students, 1970).

It was the evening of Pesach (Passover). Grandfather Abraham looked around the table at his family: his daughter Rachael, her husband David and their children. Reuben, his youngest grandson, was reciting in Hebrew the first of the four questions which the youngest child in the family traditionally recites every Seder:

'Why is this night different from all other nights?'

His mind went back over the years to a night when he too had asked the very same questions, but how very different that night had been to this.

There had been no white tablecloth or best china then. There were no cut glasses for the wine or silver candlesticks. The beker or kiddush cup which they had used was a cracked cup containing nothing but a sip of water. There had been no smiling faces, no wine, not even any proper food.

It had been the eve of the Jewish uprising in the Warsaw ghetto. The year was 1943. News had reached them that the Nazis were moving in to kill what were left of the Warsaw Jews: a mere twelve or fourteen thousand – no-one knew the exact count – out of what had been a population of half a million. Abraham could still remember the horror of the two and a half years he had spent in the ghetto: people dying in the streets of starvation; how they had to live in the sewers hidden away from the Nazi soldiers to escape capture; the filth, the sickness, and the rats ...

David was now breaking the matzot and would hide a half [called the 'afikomen'] for the children to find. Abraham remembered that there had been no matzot, no unleavened bread, at that dreadful Seder in 1943. When some of the grown-ups had questioned this because it was against Jewish law, their rabbi had explained that the Lord never asked his people to keep laws that would lead to their death. The saving of life was the most important commandment of all to God, the Creator of all life. Then the rabbi had recited a prayer:

'Behold, we are prepared and ready to fulfil Your commandment "And you shall live by them and not die by them ...". Therefore our prayer to You is that You may keep us alive and save us and rescue us speedily.'

Then he had continued, just as David was doing now,

'This is the bread of affliction which our fathers ate in the land of Egypt. Let all those who are hungry come in and partake.' The bread that had been passed round was hard and stale but it was the only thing Abraham had to eat that day.

So the Seder, then and now, followed its traditional pattern, as it did every year. When, on that April night in 1943, they had reached the part 'Next year in Jerusalem ...', there were tears in Abraham's mother's eyes. She had known, as all the grown-ups had known, that for many of them there would be no next year. They would die defending the ghetto tomorrow or, if they survived, die later in the Nazi death camps.

The rabbi had related the story of the first Exodus, when the Jews had been slaves in Egypt and God had sent Moses to lead them to freedom. As he listened, Abraham had understood that this was not just a story belonging to past history. It was *his* story. It was the story of the Jews in all ages. It was the story of *all* who struggled to be free. He nodded to himself as he recalled those time-honoured words of the Seder:

'It is our duty to thank, praise, laud, glorify, exalt, honour, bless and extol Him who wrought all these miracles for our fathers and for us. He brought us forth from bondage to freedom, from grief to joy, from mourning to festivity, from darkness to great light, and from subjection to redemption. Let us, therefore, sing before Him. Hallelujah. Praise the Lord.'

Abraham looked up at his family again and smiled, for he had truly come from grief to joy. The bondage and suffering of those horror-filled years of war had given way to the freedom and festivity which he now enjoyed. He joined his gruff and wavering voice to the shrill trebles of his grandchildren as they sang their favourite Pesach song: 'Dayenu. It is enough.'

Dayenu

At the conclusion of the Seder it is customary to sing special psalms known as the Hallel (Hallelujah) Psalms and other songs, with varying degrees of seriousness. Each family will have its particular favourites but 'Dayenu' is among the most popular.

> God has done many things for the Jewish people.
> He brought them out of Egypt.
> He helped them cross the Red Sea.
> He gave them Shabbat.
> He gave them the Torah.
> They sing Dayenu to thank Him:
> 'It would have been enough.'
>
> If God had brought us out of Egypt,
> Had he split the waters for us,
> Had he led us through on dry land, Dayenu.
>
> **Chorus**
> Da-da-ye-nu *(three times)*
> Dayenu *(twice)*
> Dayenu *(twice)*
> *(Repeat)*
>
> If God had given us the Sabbath *(twice)*,
> But had not brought us to Mount Sinai, Dayenu.
>
> If God had given us His Torah *(twice)*,
> But had not brought us into our own land, Dayenu.
>
> If God had brought us into Israel *(twice)*,
> But had not built for us the Temple, Dayenu.
>
> Had He built for us the Temple *(twice)*,
> And not sent us prophets of truth, Dayenu.
>
> Had he sent us prophets of truth *(twice)*,
> And not given us the synagogue, Dayenu.
>
> Had he given us the synagogue
> And not sent us to the nations
> To proclaim His unity, Dayenu.
>
> Had he sent us to the nations
> To proclaim His unity
> And not raised up scholars and saints, Dayenu.

THE AFFECTIVE APPROACH

One area which many teachers find difficult is how to approach the spiritual dimension in a child's education. Spirituality cannot be taught. The most we can do is to create space for reflection and to encourage children to explore for themselves questions about life and death, good and bad – those areas which go beyond the purely factual.

Artefacts can be used in this context as a focus for thoughts. Concentrating hard on one object can quieten a class and make a pause in the busy school day. It is surprising how often we fill our days and those of the children we teach with activity and noise, and do not allow or encourage a more reflective environment. The type of activity explored in this chapter gives children room to think.

The sample activity described here uses a reflective or meditative approach as an introduction to a theme: understanding the significance of light in religion. The advantage of such an approach is that it enables teachers who are unfamiliar with this method to try it out in a structured and focused way. There is always a danger of reflective exercises being too wishy-washy and lacking in focus. This is usually because teachers have not thought through their aims and objectives clearly enough first nor structured the lesson tightly enough. The approach proposed also helps to safeguard against some of the dangers highlighted in the following section.

Do's and Don'ts

Some people may be uneasy about the sample activity because they find it similar to meditation. They may be worried that children are too suggestible and there is a danger that the teacher is indoctrinating them. It is important, therefore, to keep the activity open. We have to be clear in our aims yet allow the children to follow their own thoughts.

Any suggestions or guidance must conform to generally accepted values of school or society. Similar types of activity are sometimes employed in PSE or moral-education lessons. Here there have been cases where pupils have been asked to focus on 'unhappy' thoughts with unexpected and traumatic results. For this reason I always concentrate on positive values and ideas, since my aim is not to explore the psyche of my pupils but to give them an opportunity to experience a sense of quiet and relaxation. With older pupils this may extend to a tiny insight into the *techniques* of meditation used by some religious groups but *not* to the content of those meditations.

Always ask yourself if the artefacts and activity you have chosen would compromise any child in the class. For example, focusing on a Madonna and Child might be acceptable in a Roman Catholic school but not in a school with a high Muslim intake. The sample activity uses a candle (or nightlight) for its focus. This a neutral artefact that belongs to many religions and to none. Therefore it is unlikely to raise problems of appropriateness.

Preliminary Sessions

For this type of activity to succeed, it is essential that the whole class is willing to cooperate and participate in the venture. It takes only one child to disrupt the rest and make it impossible to continue. Because children may feel uncomfortable with the silence and 'space', it may be helpful to build up to the reflective lesson with short practice sessions, perhaps at the beginning or end of the day or after the lunch break.

Many children respond positively to contracts and understand that if they cooperate they will be able to try a new activity or do something they really enjoy. They often respond to a challenge too, such as 'This is very difficult and you will need to try hard if you are going to succeed.' It goes without saying that any modicum of success will be praised to encourage further effort.

These are the stages which I have found work well in these preliminary sessions:

STAGE 1: Encourage the children to think about how they are sitting. If they are seated on a chair, make sure their feet are both flat on the floor and their spines are well supported. Legs should not be crossed.

Ask them to close their eyes and imagine a thread tied to their head, pulling them taller. When they are 'sitting tall', get them to shrug their shoulders down, with their hands hanging by their sides. Then they should shake their hands until they feel heavy, when they should be lightly placed in their lap. The first time the children need hold this position for only a few seconds. If they have coped easily so far you could proceed directly to Stage 2.

Young children may feel comfortable sitting cross-legged on the floor or even in the lotus position. They can pick up the exercise from the 'thread on the head'.

STAGE 2: Next session, repeat Stage 1, which shouldn't take as long this time, then get the children to think about their breathing. Ask them to breathe in to the count of three, hold the breath for three, breathe out for three and hold again for three. This slows down the breathing but the count should be at a comfortable pace and not too slow, especially for young children. Once all are breathing to this rhythm, they can concentrate on how their body reacts, i.e. their chest should expand on breathing in and contract on breathing out. They can feel this by placing their hands on their diaphragm.

Another breathing technique is to imagine breathing in cool, fresh air and then breathing warm air out to all parts of the body, relaxing them and making them feel heavy.

The children could also try stretching each part of the body in turn starting with the feet: stretch and relax, stretch and relax.

STAGE 3: Repeat Stages 1 and 2 then move on to focusing exercises. Try listening to all the sounds you can hear in the classroom and outside. An extension of this would be to listen to a tape of music or other sounds, e.g. waves on the seashore. Another focusing exercise is to listen to a story or a guided fantasy, where the children imagine finding a precious object, for example.

It is important that the teacher **brings the pupils round slowly** at the end of each session. A good way to do this is to get them to take a deep breath when they are ready then have a good stretch before opening their eyes.

Feedback after each session is also useful as it indicates how the children felt and what did or did not work for them. Each group of children will be different.

EXAMPLE: A Flame as a Focus for Reflection

AIM: To encourage children to reflect upon the meanings that light has for them.

This lesson could be used as an introduction to studying one or more of the festivals of light, such as Divali, Hanukkah, Christmas or Easter. Alternatively, it could be part of an exploration of religious symbolism and symbolic language.

OBJECTIVES:
- To give each child an opportunity for quiet reflection and practising this skill
- To draw on the children's own experience of light and its associations for them
- To broaden their understanding of the significance of light through shared experience and ideas

Focusing and Reflecting on a Flame

Resources	• Candles and holders/sand or nightlights • Chalkboard or flipchart

Pupil Response	Activity
	Put the children into small groups – four is an ideal size – and sit them around a candle or nightlight. If you can darken the room, so much the better. Once the children are all settled, start the relaxation exercises above with eyes closed.
Responding Being still	Light the candles then ask the children to open their eyes and concentrate hard on the flame, shutting out everything else. Teachers may want to prompt pupils to think about shape, colours or movement to help them in this.
Cooperating Participating	After a few minutes, ask the children to rub their hands hard together, creating warmth from the friction, then cup their hands over their open eyes, a technique known as 'palming'. This is restful for the eyes and also reduces the temptation to look around. It encourages the pupils to shut out other images and creates a safe, warm feeling. (Pupils wearing glasses should remove them before rubbing their hands together.)
Remembering Imagining	Next ask the children to recall the image of the flame behind their eyes.* As they are doing this, get them to think about what the candle reminds them of.
Responding Brainstorming	After a few minutes let them open and uncover their eyes then encourage them to brainstorm as a class all the words, things, feelings which the flame reminded them of. Children should be free to respond as they wish. The list can be wide ranging and at this stage everything can be included without comment. If the teacher is afraid that some children might opt out or be shy, pupils can be asked to write down their own list of words first, before sharing them with the rest of the class in the brainstorm.

A typical list produced by the brainstorm might be something like this:

• light	• sun	• Wee Willie	• excitement
• warmth	• Christmas	Winkie	• seeing
• birthdays	• good	• happy	• unafraid

*This technique in a more refined and developed form is known as 'visualization' and is employed in some forms of Buddhist meditation as a means of focusing on a particular Bodhisatta. However, in this exercise any such religious content would not be appropriate.

Safety	Obviously there are safety implications in using candles, particularly with younger children. Attempt this only with a well-disciplined class. Place nightlights on saucers or stand candles in a tray of sand. Make sure that hair is kept tied back.

Follow-up Activities	• Opposites: children could add an opposite to each word on the list. • Candle poems: children could use words on the list in a poem on the subject of light. This could be displayed in the shape of a candle. • Tell a story about light. • Bring in pictures of the Amnesty International candle or, if you can do so safely, a real candle surrounded by barbed wire. (Alternatively, Amnesty International produce a candle with a barbed-wire transfer.) Use this symbol as a stimulus to discuss how it makes the children feel and/or what it is saying. Older and more able children may wish to investigate the work of Amnesty International in more detail, and discuss why the candle symbol was chosen. • Discuss the importance of light as an energy source and as a means of life (essential for plant growth). This could be linked with the Creation story found in Genesis 1, where light is the first thing which God made.

Summary	Summarizing with the children what they have learnt is important as it draws together the work so far and reinforces the lesson. Discuss first with the children why they think light is important in general. Light is important in many religions. On the basis of what they have learnt already, can the children suggest any reasons *why* light is an appropriate symbol in religion? Next, do they know of any ways in which light is used in religion? This question can lead into further research into the place of light in religion and its significance.

Some Aspects of World Religions where Light Plays an Important Part

Buddhism	Enlightenment of the Buddha FESTIVAL: Wesak
Christianity	Jesus, Light of the World Holy Spirit God as fire FESTIVALS: Advent, Christmas, Easter
Hinduism	Light overcomes darkness Light as a welcome FESTIVAL: Divali
Islam	Star and crescent as symbols of Allah as a light guiding Muslims through life, as the moon and stars guided the first Muslims across the desert
Judaism	Menorah (seven-branched candlestick) Hanukiah (nine-branched candlestick) Shabbat (Sabbath) candles Ner Tamid, the Everlasting Light that burns above the Aron Hakodesh (Holy Ark) in the synagogue Torah as a light guiding Jews through life FESTIVAL: Hanukkah
Sikhism	FESTIVAL: Divali, but note that Sikhs celebrate the release from prison of the Sixth Guru, Har Gobind, at Divali, not the return home of the Hindu deities Rama and Sita

Other Ideas for an Affective Approach

Other items suitable for this approach include objects from nature (not strictly artefacts because not manufactured), e.g. a seed, flower, sea-shell. These objects can be used in a similar way to the candle flame as a means of focusing attention. The pupils are settled as above then directed to open their eyes and concentrate on the object in front of them. They can be asked to observe its shape, texture, design, colours, etc. After a few moments the object is removed and the pupils are asked to describe what they have seen in as much detail as possible.

The aim of such exercises is to encourage the children to look more closely at their world and to appreciate its wonder and beauty. Using naturally occurring objects in this way could be an introduction to themes such as creation, creation stories or caring for our world. It could also provide a focus for a guided fantasy where a suitable piece of writing or a story encourages the children to use their imagination to explore the theme.

A similar activity might be attempted with a specifically religious artefact. In this case the artefact could be used to focus the attention whilst a story about the artefact or the person or deity it represents is read out loud. Here the best stories are those which refer to particular aspects of the artefact which the children can observe for themselves.

Music can be used in a similar way to natural objects to explore feelings and emotions and as a background to a piece of meditative (reflective) writing read by the teacher. Music, however, has to be selected with great care since tastes vary considerably both between adults and between young and older people! What to the teacher may be a beautiful, peaceful and evocative piece of music may be boring and meaningless, even incomprehensible, to a young child. Try to judge 'where the children are at' first so that you have some idea of the likely response to the music you have chosen.

Adapted versions of exercises of this type could be used in collective worship, provided that the artefact is large enough for all the children to see reasonably well.

Resources on Light

Advent, Christmas, Chanukah, Divali, Easter, Festivals of the Buddha, Living Festivals Series (RMEP). Books on festivals of light for secondary pupils, but also useful for teacher reference.

Don't Just Do Something, Sit There, by Mary K. Stone (RMEP). A teacher's handbook on using reflective techniques, relaxation and guided fantasy for spiritual development.

CHILDREN'S FICTION:
Can't You Sleep, Little Bear? by M. Waddell and B. Firth (Walker).
The Park in the Dark, by M. Waddell and B. Firth (Walker).
After Dark, by Louis Baum (Magnet).
Moonshine, by Jan Ormerod (Picture Puffin).
The Owl Who Was Afraid of the Dark, by Jill Tomlinson (Puffin).

ADDRESS:
Amnesty International (British Section), 99–119 Rosebery Avenue, London EC1R 4RE. (Tel. 0171-278-600; fax. 0171-833-1510)

STORY

In the Dark

Everything looked strange. Peter strained his eyes in the blackness but all he could see was dark shapes. This was the first night in their new home – the first time that Peter had had a bedroom of his very own. He had spent a busy day helping to unpack his toys and arrange his books on the shelves. It had been so exciting, but now ...

He glanced over at where he thought the chair was, but in its place was a broad-shouldered creature with a pointed hat. It looked just like the ugly troll from *The Three Billy Goats Gruff*, which Peter had been reading just before his mum had turned the light off.

Peter turned his back and pulled the bedclothes tighter around him. He peered out from under them at the window, only that was worse! There was someone with long, bony fingers tapping at the glass, someone trying to get in. An owl screeched and somewhere in the distance he could hear a dog howling.

Now he heard the stairs creak under a slow, deliberate tread. The sound was getting closer. Peter could stand it no longer.

'Mum!' he cried in terror. 'Mu-u-u-m!'

The door burst open and the switch was flicked. Light flooded the room and there was his mum standing in the doorway. She was holding a mug full of warm milk which she had carried carefully up the stairs to avoid spilling any.

'Whatever is the matter, Peter?' she asked. 'You were shouting the house down. You'll wake Emma. Are you hurt?'

Peter blinked in the sudden light and looked around his room. He saw the old chair with the big stuffed clown which his sister Emma had left behind. He got out of bed and went to the window. There was the old oak tree, its branches twisted and shaped like fingers which tapped gently against the window when the wind blew.

Peter laughed. 'No, Mum. There's nothing to be afraid of.' He took the milky drink from his mum and snuggled down into his bed once more.

'Night, Mum,' he called. 'Oh, and can you leave the landing light on when you go downstairs, please,' he added. 'Just to make sure.'

9 BUILDING AND USING COLLECTIONS OF ARTEFACTS

Where to Begin

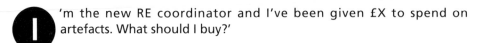

'm the new RE coordinator and I've been given £X to spend on artefacts. What should I buy?'

This, or something along these lines, is one of the questions that I'm most frequently asked. There is no instant answer but there are basic guidelines teachers can follow to help them choose the items that will be best for their school:

1. Which religions will you be teaching and resourcing? If you are in any doubt on this, look at your local Agreed Syllabus or 5–14 Document (Scotland). It goes without saying that there is little point in spending precious funds on an area the school will not be covering!

2. Within the religions studied, what areas will be focused on? Again, there is no point, for example, buying a Seder plate if there are no plans to teach anything about Jewish festivals. Thus the next stage is to look closely at the programmes of study for RE for your school to gain a more-detailed idea of the areas which will be covered. If programmes of study have not yet been written, it will be advisable to postpone your final decision on which artefacts to buy until they have been completed.

3. With the programmes of study in mind, consider how artefacts might be used **as one of a range of different strategies** to deliver the content and achieve the aims and objectives of your syllabus. The focus in this book is on artefacts but check that overall your RE methodology is varied and balanced in terms of, for example, active/passive, group/individual, oral/written, factual/creative activities. (Active activities include discussion, debate, ranking, making, role-play/drama, brainstorming, visits and visitors. Passive activities include watching videos and listening.) This is also the stage at which some thought should be given to the what and how of assessment.

Within these strategies there should be plenty of room for introducing artefacts in a creative and effective way. It is hoped that the previous chapters will spur on the imagination and open up for the teacher abundant possibilities. (See also the basic collections of artefacts for different faiths listed on pages 64–73.) Artefacts have the most effect when used in a range of different ways. Thus each artefact activity should be an integral part of a complete and planned teaching programme, not just an interesting afterthought.

Once the basic draft of the programmes of study is in place and a short list of artefacts required has been drawn up, there are a few further points which need to be considered. Several of the following are not restricted to selecting artefacts but apply to other resources as well.

1. Will each artefact accurately reflect the religion pupils are studying? It is important to ensure that all items are mainstream and authentic, but much will also depend on the way they are presented and used in the classroom. Some artefacts (e.g. a Muslim prayer-mat) may not be so important in themselves but can be used to demonstrate a fundamental concept (e.g. the importance of daily prayer in Islam). Teachers should be aware themselves if this is the case and make it clear to colleagues and pupils to avoid misrepresentation and misunderstandings. Similarly, teachers need to be alert to the danger of inadvertantly stereotyping a faith or its members, e.g. by giving pupils the (wrong) impression that all male Jews wear kippahs.

2. Will your choice of artefacts give maximum teaching value? Can some items be used in a variety of ways: for example, to stimulate interest, as part of a display, to explore the affective/spiritual dimension, to illustrate a story? Can items be used on their own or will some require supplementary resources?

3. Will your artefact collection have sufficient variety? Will it, as a collection, appeal to all the senses: touch, smell, sight, hearing, taste?

4. Will there be a balance within each religion, e.g. will your Christian artefacts reflect Orthodox, Roman Catholic and Non-conformist denominations? Some religious traditions are far richer in artefacts than others. This may lead to a preponderance of items from a particular tradition at the expense of other traditions within the same religion. In this case, teachers will need to find alternative ways of redressing the balance, perhaps through the use of music, pictures or videos to achieve a fair representation of the faith as a whole.

Beware also of presenting a Eurocentric or nationalist view of any faith, e.g. looking only at Western Christianity, or giving the impression that all Jews live in Israel or all Muslims come from Pakistan. Religious practice often reflects the culture of the country in which the faith has rooted.

5. Will there be a balance in terms of cost, materials and aesthetic value? Inevitably, cost is going to be an important consideration, but try to put together a collection of artefacts ranging from the cheap to the more expensive.

Classroom artefacts will need to be supplemented by videos, posters, pictures, photographs, etc., so that pupils become aware of the diversity and richness of the religious artistic tradition. At the same time, it is important to remember that cheaper artefacts that appear unappealing to some may accurately reflect a group within a tradition. For example, a plastic Lourdes water-bottle in the form of the Immaculate Conception may not be to everyone's taste, yet that very same item is bought by thousands of Roman Catholics every year when they go to Lourdes on pilgrimage. In a similar way, many Hindu homes possess colourful plastic images of deities. These represent their social, cultural and economic background. It would be as false to deny that these artefacts are important as to forget the great artistic achievements which fashioned the amazing Hindu temples of India or gave us the breathtaking ceiling of the Sistine Chapel. As Patricia Bahree Barylski wrote:

> 'We view art [and artefacts] through a set of assumptions. Our reaction is shaped by our world view ...', and perhaps even more telling, 'The assumed superiority of all things Western that went hand in hand with colonialism also hampered clear vision.'

> (Article on art and the Hindu tradition in *World Religions in Education 1991–1992*, Shap Mailing)

Children should be encouraged to appreciate that there are different ideas about what is beautiful and that these may be affected by culture, age, taste and experience. We need to learn not to make hasty judgements about things which don't immediately appeal to a Western eye.

6. Have any possible areas of sensitivity been identified and will they be adequately addressed? (See Chapter 2, pages 11–13, for general guidance and 'Do's and Don'ts' sections in other chapters for more details.)

7. Have issues of safety been considered? What needs to be done to overcome potential dangers? (See also pages 13–14.)

If you need help or independent advice, contact your local RE inspector or adviser. He or she will be able to give you guidance on programmes of study, INSET courses and where to obtain artefacts.

Many RE coordinators add to artefact collections a few helpful books, their own notes or maybe some teaching plans and suggestions to assist those teachers who are feeling unsure at first. As with all the National Curriculum subjects, most teachers will quickly gain confidence and enthusiasm once they've had a bit of experience and practice. A few INSET sessions can be great confidence-boosters too. If teachers can be encouraged to add their own comments and worksheets to the collections as they use them this will be an additional help to others. It will also enable the RE coordinator to review the effectiveness of particular artefacts. Evidence of a well-used set of artefacts can be useful ammunition when applying for funding!

Cataloguing and Storage

Once the artefacts arrive in school they will need to be catalogued in some way. It is important that all religious artefacts are carefully stored, with proper respect, and that they are easily accessible to all members of staff if they are to be fully utilized. It is a good idea to keep items from the same religion together in one box. Colour-coding is a ideal way of achieving this, particularly if the code is extended to labelling too. Alternatively you may decide to build up 'theme' boxes based on concepts such as celebrations or festivals or clothes. Involving pupils in the cataloguing and labelling of the collections encourages them to learn respect and care for the items, as well as assisting hard-pressed teachers.

Another attractive possibility is an artefact trolley, consisting of six deep, colour-coded drawers which will hold six collections of artefacts and/or some books. Trolleys on castors can be wheeled from classroom to classroom, a real asset in primary schools where the artefacts are borrowed by all members of staff and there is no RE room in which to store them. The flat trolley top can double as an artefact display area too.

Whatever system of storage and access is decided upon, it should be agreed by all members of staff and then maintained, otherwise artefacts will not be available when required.

A list of the artefacts should be included in each box or drawer. Since many primary teachers have little (or even no) specialist knowledge of RE, brief notes on what each artefact is, its significance and any areas of sensitivity of which teachers need to be aware would be most helpful. If individual items are coded in any way this should be done discreetly, preferably out of sight on the base or reverse side. It should always be remembered that some artefacts are sacred to some believers and we should avoid defacing them in any way.

| Buy, Borrow or Share? | Many schools and some local education authorities make available 'one-off' allocations of money for starting an artefact collection. If your budget isn't big enough for your requirements, list the artefacts you have chosen and make a case for why you need them. If this fails to produce additional funds, prioritize your requirements to fit the budget. |

Before you buy anything, however, check to see how much you can cadge or borrow from:

- local churches and other places of worship;
- parents;
- RE centres, libraries and education-authority resource bases.

Remember, however, that if items are borrowed they will have to be returned. They may therefore not be available when needed or for as long as they are required. There may also be problems over borrowing 'seasonal' artefacts from a resource base, as demand for them is likely to be highest around the time of the festival they're linked to. It may make more sense to buy these items and borrow the 'unseasonal' ones.

Some schools make their money go further by pooling resources amongst a number of schools in the same area or by sharing with the local secondary or high school. As with using resource bases, teachers may prefer to buy the cheaper and more frequently used or seasonal items and own collectively those which are more expensive. This is a creative use of limited resources and it has benefits in the sharing of ideas and forming links with other schools. It does, however, require someone to take responsibility for the collection: labelling the artefacts, checking them in and out, and generally keeping the system running smoothly.

Remember, if you can't afford everything you think you'll require, you can always start small and add to your collection over the years, as funds become available. You should also bear in mind the need for replacing damaged or lost artefacts.

Where to Buy Artefacts

Many teachers delight in visiting mosques, synagogues, temples and other places of worship where there are small shops attached or in going round 'ethnic' shops. There they will spend hours ferreting out bargains, often paying for artefacts out of their own pockets. It was for the majority of other teachers who, through shyness, lack of time or local availability or for pure ease, preferred to use a mail-order catalogue to obtain resources that I first set up Articles of Faith. Our list of customers shows that it has been a useful source for many involved in the teaching of RE at all levels.

An up-to-date catalogue can be obtained by phoning 0161-7636232, by faxing 0161-7633421 or by writing to:

Articles of Faith Ltd, REsource House, Kay Street, Bury BL9 6BU.

For those who wish to see before they buy, we also have a small training room on the premises where many of the artefacts, videos and IT programs we stock are available for inspection.

If you would like further information or advice on sources of artefacts, consult your local RE inspector or adviser.

The following sections include basic collections for each of the six major world faiths which you should be able to buy for around £50 (excluding VAT). These are collections of artefacts which I have put together for Articles of Faith. They are based on wide consultation with teachers and our experience of what have proved to be the most popular artefacts in schools. Other considerations have been price and availability.

Artefacts for a 'Festivals of Light' collection costing less than £40 are also suggested, along with ideas for other thematic collections.

These lists are **not** intended to be prescriptive nor, even with the additional items suggested, exhaustive. They are included here for general guidance only. Your own collection of artefacts should be selected **to meet the needs of your school**, bearing in mind the considerations raised earlier in this chapter.

Buddhist Artefacts

The artefact most often associated with Buddhism is a Buddha rupa, or image of the Buddha. Which rupa is chosen will partly depend on budget and availability. The more expensive ones may be more durable and give better fine detail but there are cheaper ones that are equally pleasing. If your budget allows, choose more that one rupa, representing different areas and traditions, so that similarities and differences can be looked at.

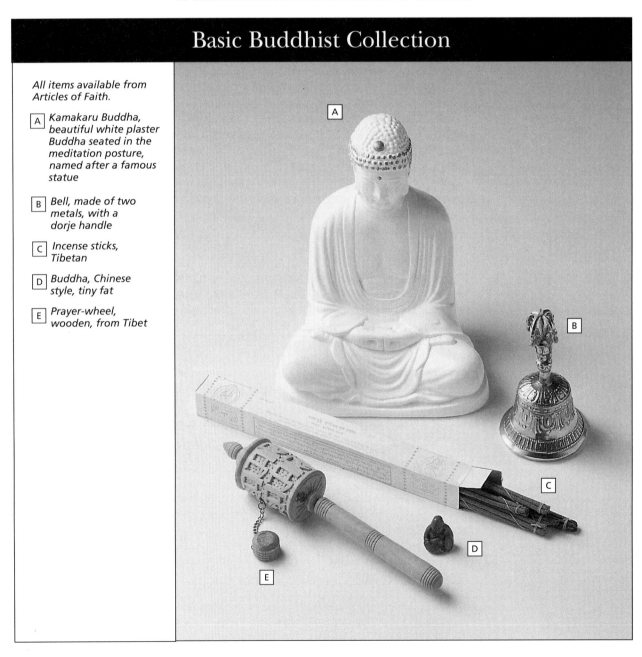

Basic Buddhist Collection

All items available from Articles of Faith.

A *Kamakaru Buddha, beautiful white plaster Buddha seated in the meditation posture, named after a famous statue*

B *Bell, made of two metals, with a dorje handle*

C *Incense sticks, Tibetan*

D *Buddha, Chinese style, tiny fat*

E *Prayer-wheel, wooden, from Tibet*

Buddha rupas which incorporate an incense-holder should be avoided, as many Buddhists find these unacceptable.

The bell illustrated comes from the Tantric (Tibetan) tradition of Buddhism. It might be used by Buddhists in puja (worship) and has symbolic significance as well. The bell represents the female aspect whilst the dorje or vajra (thunder-bolt) represents the male aspect. Dorjes are also available separately.

The prayer-wheel is also typical of the Tibetan Buddhist tradition, as are prayer-flags. The prayer-wheel illustrated is hand held and contains a mantra. It is common to see people walking along spinning wheels such as these in countries like Nepal and Tibet.

Additional Buddhist Artefacts

- Offering-bowls and incense with holder to place before a Buddha rupa (see Chapter 6).
- Monk's or nun's robe and alms-bowl, if you're going to focus on the role of monks/nuns in the Buddhist community or Sangha.
- Cloth thangka or posters of thangkas.

Christian Artefacts

Putting together a collection of Christian artefacts on a budget of £50 is quite hard, maybe because many teachers are more familiar with the full range of items available. This is an area where it is often possible to borrow artefacts, thus releasing funds for less readily obtainable items.

Basic Christian Collection

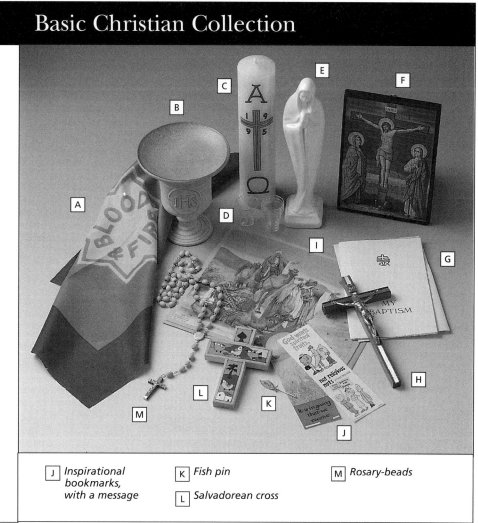

All items available from Articles of Faith.

- A *Salvation Army waving-flag*
- B *Chalice and paten, pottery*
- C *Easter (paschal) candle*
- D *Communion cups, plastic, as used in, for example, Baptist and Methodist churches*
- E *Madonna, white china*
- F *Icon, Greek*
- G *Baptism certificate, for believer's baptism*
- H *Crucifix*
- I *Advent calendar, with traditional Bible scene. (I always select calendars with religious scenes but those with secular scenes could be used for comparison.)*
- J *Inspirational bookmarks, with a message*
- K *Fish pin*
- L *Salvadorean cross*
- M *Rosary-beads*

To create a balanced Christian collection, it is necessary, first, to remember that Christianity is a worldwide faith, therefore artefacts from Christian traditions other than those in the West should be included. In the above selection the Salvadorean cross and the Greek icon fulfil this function.

The second criterion is to represent the full spectrum of Christianity. Thus the icon illustrated is Orthodox, the crucifix and rosary-beads Roman Catholic, the chalice and paten Catholic/Anglican, the Communion cups Methodist/Baptist, the flag comes from the Salvation Army and the bookmarks typically, but not invariably, from an evangelical background.

The basic collection also covers Christian festivals, through the Advent calendar and Easter candle, and the sacraments of baptism and the Eucharist (or Communion or Mass or Lord's Supper, etc.).

The fish was the earliest Christian symbol, chosen because *ichthus*, the Greek word for 'fish', is an acronym for a sentence meaning 'Jesus Christ, God's Son, Saviour'.

Additional Christian Artefacts

Schools can augment their basic collection according to the particular areas which they will be teaching, in order to present an even better balance. Different types of cross are one possibility (see Chapter 4). The dove can also be introduced when teaching about symbols or as a lead into the concept of the Holy Spirit (related themes: baptism, confirmation or Pentecost/Whitsun).

It is assumed that every school will have access to at least one Bible. If children are to read with understanding, it is advisable to have one of the modern translations available, such as the Children's International Version or the Good News Bible. In schools where there is a large non-Christian intake the former version is recommended, as some faiths are unhappy with the title of the latter and raise objections to its use.

Hindu Artefacts

The most appropriate artefacts to include in your Hindu collection will depend on the areas being taught. There is a wide range of murtis (images) of gods and goddesses to choose from, so your syllabus has to be the guide here. The collection illustrated incorporates some of the most popular Hindu deities.

Lakshmi, the consort of the god Vishnu, is the goddess of wealth and beauty. She is particularly important at Hindu New Year and the festival of Divali (in October/November), when many Hindu businesses close their books, settle their accounts and pray to her for success in the coming year. Typically, one of her hands is open in the mudra (symbolic hand position) of bounty.

Rama, Sita, Lakshman and Hanuman are four of the main characters from the Hindu epic the Ramayana, a story which is told in the period leading up to Divali. Rama and Lakshman, his brother, can be identified by the bows and quivers which they carry. Sita is Rama's beautiful wife, whom the ten-headed demon Ravana captured and carried off to the island of (Sri) Lanka. Hanuman is the monkey-king who, with his army of monkeys, helped Rama and Lakshman to rescue Sita. Rama is one of the avatars (descents, or earthly forms) of the great god Vishnu.

At Divali, diva lamps are lit to welcome home Rama and Sita, and Divali cards are sent to family and friends.

Krishna, like Rama, is an avatar of Vishnu. There are many stories told about the birth of Krishna, his mischievous childhood and the devotion of the gopis (cowgirls or milkmaids) to him, attracted by his mellifluous flute playing. The gopi Radha is his consort and her love for Krishna is seen as a symbol of the Hindu devotee's love for Lord Krishna.

Basic Hindu Collection

*All items available from
Articles of Faith.*

A *Ganesha, plastic*

B *Aum or Om symbol,
metal*

C *Rama, Sita,
Lakshman and
Hanuman, plastic*

D *Radha and Krishna,
plastic*

E *Lakshmi, plastic*

F *Joss sticks, for puja*

G *Mendhi kit,
comprising henna,
stencil and book of
designs*

H *Prayer-beads (mala)*

I *Divali card*

J *Puja set, comprising
tray, bell, tumbler
and spoon, diva lamp,
incense-holder,
container for kum
kum powder*

K *Kum kum powder*

L *Diva lamp,
decorated clay, for
Divali*

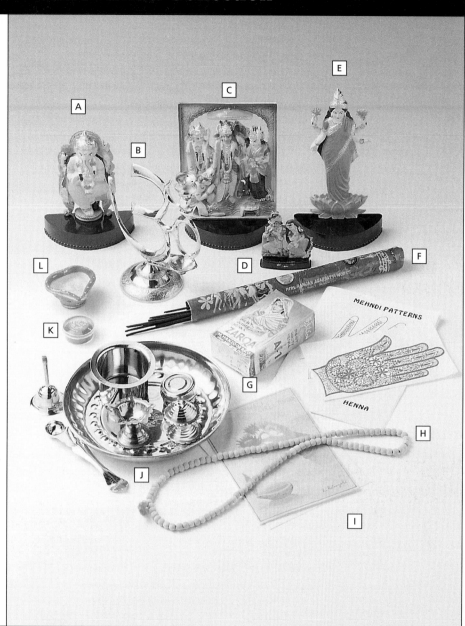

One of the best known and most popular of the Hindu scriptures, the Bhagavad Gita or Song of the Lord, is an account of a discussion on the eve of battle between Krishna, acting as charioteer, and the prince Arjuna. In it, Krishna explains the concept of karma and duty.

Ganesha is the popular elephant-headed son of the great god Shiva and his consort Parvati. He is the god of good fortune and overcomer of obstacles. His image appears on wedding cards and other invitations. Many Hindu homes have a picture or murti (statue) of him.

Aum or Om is a sacred syllable in the ancient Sanskrit language. It is often used as a symbol for Hinduism. It is a word that can represent the Supreme Being or Ultimate Reality, Brahman, and is supposed to be uttered in such a way as to make four distinct sounds: a-o-u-m. These represent the four states of consciousness – subconscious, awake, asleep, dreaming – that is, reality. Other ways of describing this are as four types of time (past, present, future, eternity) or every aspect of being (male, female, neuter, all creation) or every aspect of life (birth, life, death, moksha, i.e. liberation from the cycle of rebirth). Aum can be chanted in meditation as a mantra.

The puja tray illustrated would be used by Hindus during the daily offering of worship (puja) at a shrine in the home. Before puja begins, the worshipper will bathe, then ring a small bell to let the deity/ies know that worship is about to start. Offerings of incense may be placed in the incense-holder and water or milk will be placed in the tumbler, also as an offering. The spoon will be used for giving this to the deity or to the worshipper after it has been offered to God. Other foods may also be offered as well as flowers and puja spices (haldi).

Kum kum powder or a sandalwood paste is often placed on the centre of the forehead before worship. This is known as a tikla mark. Women may wear a kum kum spot or a bindi (a coloured spot used instead of kum kum powder or liquid) on their forehead throughout the day. This indicates God's blessing.

Mendhi (henna) is a plant which acts as a dye when powdered. It is mixed into a paste and used to decorate the hands and feet, particularly at weddings and festivals. The designs are most commonly drawn freehand but stencils can be used.

Additional Hindu Artefacts

If you wish to pursue the Hindu symbolism activity in Chapter 4, a clear murti of Vishnu will be required. Some form of Shiva, maybe with his consort Parvati or as Shiva Nataraja (Lord of the Dance), would yield another deity rich in symbolism and with associated stories. Brahma (not to be confused with Brahman, the Supreme Being) is the third of the three main gods which make up the Trimurti. Murtis of Brahma alone are rarely found but representations with Vishnu and Shiva, as the Trimurti, are available.

Jewish Artefacts

When selecting Jewish artefacts it might be helpful to remember that in Judaism it is customary to buy the very best that one can afford in matters of religion. This may mean that relatively few artefacts are bought compared with other collections costing the same amount of money. In the collection illustrated, for example, I have chosen larger replica Torah scrolls (approximately 30 cm deep) which have wooden rollers and a velvet mantle. I believe these convey the importance of the Torah by their size and beauty. Nevertheless, where budgets are tight, mini scrolls would be an acceptable alternative.

A mezuzah case containing a handwritten parchment scroll of a passage from the Torah is fixed on the doorpost of every room in a Jewish home except the toilet. Mezuzah cases are available in many different sizes, shapes and materials, from plastic to gold. Metal (though not precious metal!) will be more durable for classroom use than plastic cases. Look out for cases with symbolism as part of the decoration, as this will provide an extra teaching resource. For the case to have full impact a replica of the scroll will be needed. Although authentic scrolls are available, they should not be handled and therefore are unsuitable for school use. The facsimile featured here has the text at normal reading size and also reduced to the size used on the mezuzah scroll. This enables pupils to study the form of the Hebrew and also to appreciate the care which goes into writing the actual scrolls. The mezuzah text includes the Shema (major Jewish prayer stating belief in one God).

At primary-school level, festivals are a rich and vibrant way to approach the teaching of religion. A Seder plate represents one of the key Jewish festivals, Pesach (Passover), while a hanukiah (nine-branched candlestick) with the dreidle represents the popular winter festival of Hanukkah. (A dreidle is a top used like dice in a traditional Hanukkah game of chance.)

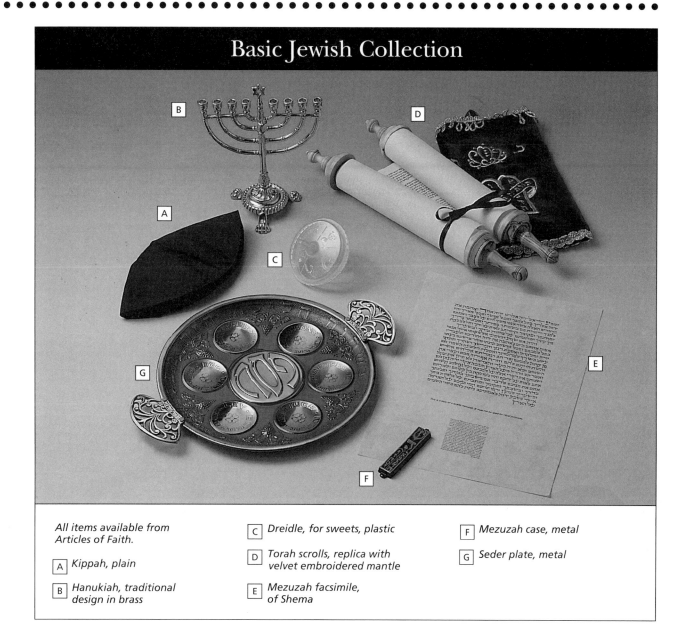

Basic Jewish Collection

All items available from Articles of Faith.

A *Kippah, plain*

B *Hanukiah, traditional design in brass*

C *Dreidle, for sweets, plastic*

D *Torah scrolls, replica with velvet embroidered mantle*

E *Mezuzah facsimile, of Shema*

F *Mezuzah case, metal*

G *Seder plate, metal*

The kippah (skull-cap) is included here as is it a commonly recognized head-covering worn by many Jewish males. However, children should be made aware that not all Jewish men wear a kippah all the time. Some wear one only at prayer. Styles and colours will also vary and special kippahs may be worn for celebrations such as a Bar Mitzvah or a wedding.

Additional Jewish Artefacts

If you intend to teach about Shabbat (the Sabbath), it would be desirable to include the artefacts placed on the Shabbat table in your collection. Several of these may be available around the home, such as a pair of candles and candle-sticks, and a wine goblet (kiddush cup). In addition a challah cloth (deke), two challot (plaited) loaves, a spice-box and a havdalah (plaited) candle with holder would complete the set.

Likewise, if you plan to set a Pesach (Passover) table, a wine goblet (kiddush cup), pair of candles and candlesticks, matzot and (matzah) cover, and a cup for Elijah would be required.

If your budget will allow, a tallit (prayer-shawl) and tefillin (small leather boxes worn on the forehead and arm) can give extra meaning and understanding to the Jewish daily prayers. Tefillin intended for classroom use should not contain scrolls (of passages from the Torah, handwritten on parchment) since it is considered inappropriate to handle these except when praying.

Muslim Artefacts

Islam is perhaps the easiest of the six major faiths for which to select a basic collection for £50 as it has fewer artefacts of a truly religious (as opposed to cultural) nature. Since prayer is one of the five duties (or pillars) of Islam, a prayer-mat, compass (used to find the direction of the Ka'bah in Makkah) and prayer-hat are obvious choices. The prayer-beads provide a balance between formal prayer (salah) and personal/intercessory prayer (du'a). They also offer the opportunity to discuss the Ninety-Nine Names of Allah.

No Muslim collection would be complete without the Qur'an in some form. A stand should also be provided so that the book can be properly and sensitively displayed.

A white robe (ihram) is worn by all male Muslims taking part in the Hajj (the annual pilgrimage to Makkah) and signifies brotherhood, equality and purity.

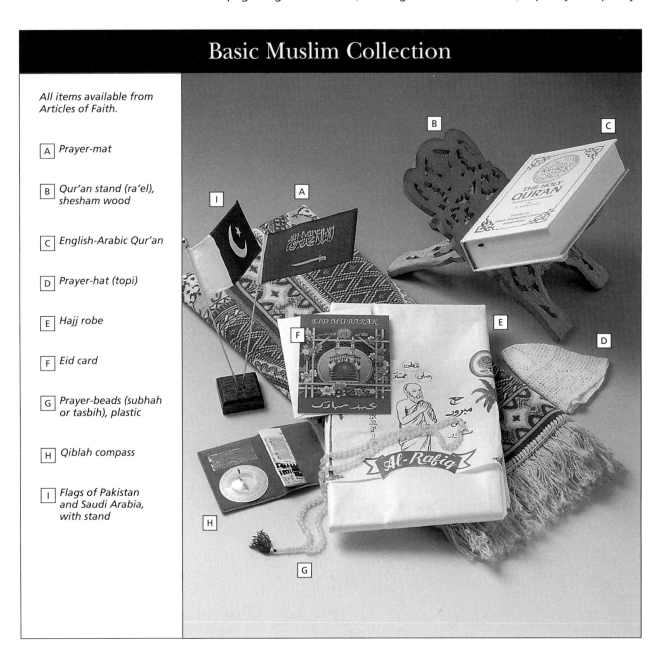

Basic Muslim Collection

All items available from Articles of Faith.

A Prayer-mat

B Qur'an stand (ra'el), shesham wood

C English-Arabic Qur'an

D Prayer-hat (topi)

E Hajj robe

F Eid card

G Prayer-beads (subhah or tasbih), plastic

H Qiblah compass

I Flags of Pakistan and Saudi Arabia, with stand

Eid (or Id) cards may be sent at either of the two main Muslim festivals, Eid-ul-Adha (held at the end of Hajj) or Eid-ul-Fitr (celebrating the end of Ramadan).

Finally, together the flags of the two Muslim countries of Pakistan and Saudi Arabia are a reminder that Islam is found in many different countries. The flag of Pakistan includes the symbol of Islam, the star and crescent, whilst the flag of Saudi Arabia bears the words of the Shahadah, 'There is no God but Allah, Muhammad is the Messenger of Allah,' and represents the first of the Five Pillars of Islam and the basic Muslim creed.

Additional Muslim Artefacts

Sikh Artefacts

Teachers could also include posters, wall-hangings or plaques, either of Qur'anic verses or of the Ka'bah in Makkah or the Prophet's Mosque in Madinah.

The basis of the collection illustrated is the Five K's:

- Kesh – uncut hair
- Kara – steel band worn on right wrist
- Kangha – comb used to keep the hair in place
- Kirpan – sword
- Kachera – special long underwear/shorts

Basic Sikh Collection

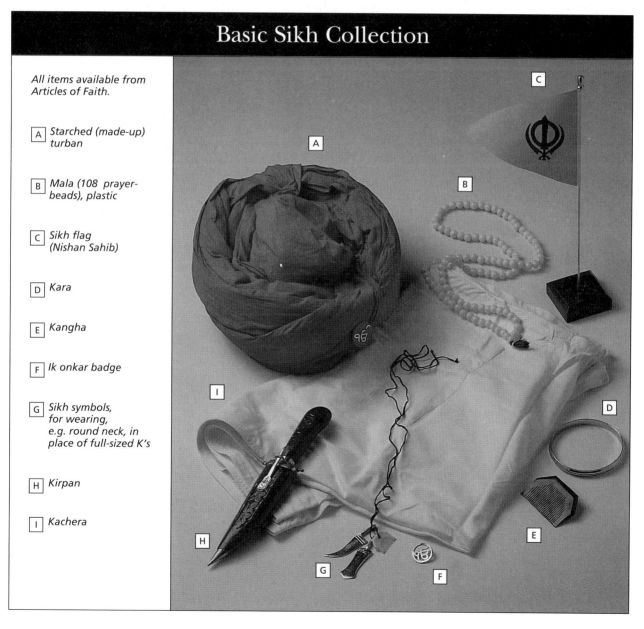

All items available from Articles of Faith.

A *Starched (made-up) turban*

B *Mala (108 prayer-beads), plastic*

C *Sikh flag (Nishan Sahib)*

D *Kara*

E *Kangha*

F *Ik onkar badge*

G *Sikh symbols, for wearing, e.g. round neck, in place of full-sized K's*

H *Kirpan*

I *Kachera*

These are the distinguishing marks of both male and female Sikhs. Not all those who call themselves Sikh will necessarily wear all the Five K's, but generally those who have undergone the Amrit ceremony of initiation into the Khalsa (the fellowship of pure Sikhs) will wish to do so.

A Sikh man usually wears a turban to keep his uncut hair in place and to identify himself as a Sikh. Teachers will have to decide for themselves whether they wish to use a starched and made-up turban, bearing in mind that not all Sikhs are happy for these to be on display in schools, either because they personally are against the wearing of ready-made turbans or because they are afraid that they will be seen as objects of ridicule. The latter reason may also be a consideration regarding the kachera. A swatch of long dark hair, a diagram of how to tie a turban and a good photograph of a Sikh wearing the Five K's would be possible alternatives.

Another consideration when putting together a Sikh artefact collection is the question of safety regarding the kirpan. Kirpans are available as full-sized swords or as smaller, 15–20 cm versions. Both are potentially dangerous if not handled properly. Teachers should point out to children that it is offensive to Sikhs to unsheathe a kirpan as it is intended for use only in defence, and is never regarded as an offensive weapon. Even so, it maybe advisable to super-glue the blade within the sheath to avoid any high-spirited or naughty youngster misusing it. Some Sikhs prefer to wear small symbolic representations of the kirpan and kangha on a chain around the neck.

'Ik onkar', meaning 'There is One God', is the first phrase in the Mool Mantra, the statement of Sikh belief that begins the Guru Granth Sahib. The badge illustrated shows 'Ik onkar' in Gurmukhi, the script in which Punjabi, the language of the Guru Granth Sahib, is written. 'Ik onkar', along with names for God such as 'Raheguru' (Wonderful Lord), can be used to illustrate the Sikh concept of God, and linked to the use of mala in prayer.

The Sikh flag can provide an introduction to the gurdwara (Sikh temple), since it always flies outside to identify the building. Also, changing the cloth that covers the flagpole is an important part of Baisakhi (the spring festival celebrating the formation of the Khalsa).

The use in the classroom of a number of artefacts from this collection at the same time makes sense. For example:

- It can introduce the idea of a 'Sikh' and thus explain the origins of Sikhism by showing how a Sikh (follower) is one who is identified by the Five K's which he or she wears.
- It can illustrate the Baisakhi story (see pages 74–76) and the founding of the Khalsa.
- It can be part of a unit of work on symbols, especially the Sikh flag and the Five K's.

Additional Sikh Artefacts

- A rumal – the head-covering worn by Sikh boys before they are old enough to tie their own turbans and by Sikh sportsmen.
- Something to represent the Guru Granth Sahib (see pages 32–33), e.g. a rumala (covering for it), or copies of sections from it such as the Japji Sahib or its opening, the Mool Mantra, or a chauri – a handle with a swatch of hair which is waved over the Guru Granth Sahib as a symbol of its authority and a mark of respect. (NB A chauri should never be referred to as a 'fly-whisk'.)
- Pictures of the Gurus, especially Guru Nanak and Guru Gobind Singh. Careful consideration must be given as to whether or not also to include statues of the Gurus. They are available and used by some Sikhs, though an

increasing number are against them because of a fear that they might lead to worship of the statues themselves and not the One True God to whom they point.

- Pictures of Amritsar, particularly the Golden Temple, the most sacred place and major pilgrimage site of Sikhism.
- Tapes of Sikh religious music (not strictly artefacts, of course!). Some schools may be able to gain access to Sikh musical instruments such as a harmonium, tabor and sitar.

Thematic Collections

The following collection containing the major artefacts associated with the three winter festivals of Advent, Divali and Hanukkah could be put together for less that £40:

ADVENT:
- Angel chimes, with four candles which when lit 'drive' a rotating angel sounding chimes
- Advent calendar
- Toctos, a small clay Nativity scene from S. America
- Christingle and Advent candles
- Christmas cards, including Third World design

At a Christingle service, the candle (representing Jesus as the Light of the World) is placed in a orange representing the Earth.

DIVALI:
- Diva lamp, clay
- Divali card
- Lakshmi, plastic

HANUKKAH:
- Hanukiah
- Hanukkah card
- Dreidle, plastic, for sweets

Other subjects which lend themselves to thematic collections include:

- Clothes (Remember that although some garments may be worn for cultural rather than religious reasons, they may nevertheless illustrate a religious concept, e.g. a Muslim headscarf indicates the Islamic belief that a woman should be modestly dressed.)
- Festivals
- Food
- Holy books and sacred writings
- Pilgrimage (journeys)
- Places of worship
- Prayer and worship
- Rites of passage: birth, initiation, marriage, death
- Symbols

In thematic teaching, careful consideration should be given to the differences between the religions included. Often apparently similar artefacts in a thematic collection may be totally different in purpose and concept, and this can lead to misunderstandings and confusion on the part of children (and sometimes teachers too!). For example, the 'food' (bread and sometimes wine) taken in a Roman Catholic Mass bears no resemblance to the symbolic foods of Pesach (Passover). To a Catholic the bread becomes in some mysterious way the actual body of Christ, thereby transcending the symbolic and encapsulating a deep theological concept. Pesach foods are rich in symbolism and give an important insight into the Jewish understanding of the nature of God and his purpose for his people, but they nevertheless remain simply food.

In considering festivals of light, the link is the symbolism of light and the triumph of good over evil. Thus Rama defeats the wicked demon Ravana in the Divali story, the Jews overcome the Greeks and rededicate the Temple in the Hanukkah story, and the Christmas story tells of the birth of Jesus, who came to conquer sin and death according to Christian theology. However teachers should be aware that although these festivals have some similarities (light, overcoming of evil, celebrated in winter), the central theologies which underlie them are very different.

STORY

A Faith to Die For

The following story is based on an actual historical event: the founding of the Sikh Khalsa. The story-teller and his wife, Ranjit, are fictional but the rest of the characters are real.

At that time the Hindu caste system was stricly adhered to. Babies were born into a caste, and lived, worked, were married and died within that caste. Today that rigid social system is beginning to break down owing to the efforts of people like Mahatma Gandhi. It was he, for example, who banned the system of outcastes (now forbidden by Indian law). Teachers should ensure that their pupils are aware that the Hindu caste system as described in this story is not an accurate description of modern Hindu practice, particularly in the West.

Was it a miracle? Some people say it was, others that it was just a clever stage show. For myself, I don't know. I can only tell you what I saw. The year was 1699, the place Anandpur [in the north of India]. It was a Hindu spring festival day and I'd gone with my wife, Ranjit, to the celebrations.

Now we are outcastes. That is, we don't belong to any of the four main Hindu castes. Some people call us Untouchables, for that's what we are. We get all the nasty jobs, the unclean jobs, like collecting the night-soil and removing dead bodies, so no-one will touch us. Perhaps our families won't live like this for ever, but right now [he means three hundred years ago] we're the lowest of the low here.

Anyway, we thought that if we kept ourselves to ourselves perhaps we'd not be noticed in the crowds, and that's what happened. What an occasion! There were stalls selling hot spicy foods, others with wonderful sticky sweets, some selling brightly coloured bangles and others with beautiful gauzy dupattas for women to wear. There were acrobats and jugglers, everywhere busy and full of life.

As we were wandering around, we saw that lots of people were moving along to an open space with a sort of raised platform at one end. We were curious, and not wanting to miss a thing, we drifted in that direction and found a spot where we could see what was going on without being noticed ourselves.

We soon realized that this was a gathering of Sikhs, followers of religious leaders called Gurus [teachers]. Now I know a bit about these people. I've been to their temples sometimes. They have a free kitchen [or langar] which is open to all and there's been many a time when I've been glad of a plate of dhal and chapatti there. They also say that everyone is equal: you can see the attraction of that for someone like me, who's at the bottom of everyone's list!

As Ranjit and I watched, the Sikh leader Guru Gobind Rai rode up on a white horse and dismounted onto the platform. He was a tall, noble-looking fellow with his bow and quiver of arrows slung over his back. There was an expectant hush as the crowd waited for him to speak. They wouldn't have been so keen if

they had known what he was going to say, I can tell you! He stood there as bold as brass and shouted to the crowd:

'Is there anyone here who is willing to give his life for his faith?'

Some people shouted 'Yeah' and others laughed, but a few, the thoughtful ones, looked puzzled and waited quietly. The Guru held up his hands:

'I mean it. Is there anyone here who is willing to die for his faith? If so, let that person come forward.'

That did it. We all knew he meant it. The laughter died away. There was nervous whispering. No-one came forward.

The Guru just stood there. His gaze swept the crowd. He had the sort of eyes that when he looked at you, you felt he knew everything you were thinking. What was going to happen? What would he do next? Suddenly there was a muttering in the crowd. Someone was pushing his way to the front. I couldn't see him clearly but the whisper soon spread among the crowd that he was from Lahore, Daya Ram by name.

The Guru put his hand on Daya Ram's left shoulder and looked at him intently. He spoke quietly to him, but no-one else could hear what he said. Daya Ram bowed his head, then he raised it and looked the Guru straight in the eye. I think I saw a slight nod of his head then the Guru led him out of sight.

We were all wondering what was going on but we didn't have to wait long. Suddenly a loud gasp went up. The Guru had returned alone but what was so terrifying was the long sword dripping with bright-red blood that he held in his hand. And he hadn't finished yet. He repeated the same challenge:

'Is there anyone here who is willing to give his life for his faith?'

Well, I don't need to tell you that no-one laughed this time. We were too stunned, shocked beyond belief. I noticed a few people beginning to drift away. Perhaps they thought the Guru was mad or dangerous. Then another man volunteered. We learnt later that he was called Dharam Das, a Jat [farmer] from Delhi.

The whole terrible scene was played out again while we watched in disbelief, but it still wasn't the end. The Guru did it again and again and again, five times in all, each time the same. At one point Ranjit put her hand on my arm as if to stop me. I ask you, do I look like a martyr? But then neither did they. I mean, washermen, water-carriers and barbers are not exactly from the noble castes – no offence intended – but that's what the last three men were. Anyway, I wasn't about to offer my head for anyone.

So, when the Guru reached five he stopped. Then, lo and behold, he went behind the screen and reappeared with the five men alive and well with not a mark on them.

'These,' he said, 'are my Panj Piare, my Five Beloved Ones. They will be the start of a new group of Sikhs, the Khalsa. You will always recognize who the members of the Khalsa are by these five things:

'They will never cut their hair – that's kesh – and will keep it in place with a kangha, a comb. They will wear a strong steel bangle, a kara, to remind them that they are united and that God is One. They must be warriors, ready to fight to defend the right of anyone, Sikh, Muslim or Hindu, to believe. A kirpan, a sword, will be a symbol of this readiness, so will shorts, kachera. These will replace our traditional clothes so that we can ride into battle on horseback more easily. These Five K's will be the mark of all those who have been initiated into [made members of] the Khalsa, as I now initiate my Panj Piare.'

So saying he gave them each a special sugary drink called Amrit. He said a lot more things too but the bit I liked best was when he declared that all people were equal. To prove the point, all the Sikh men would have the same name, Singh (which means 'lion'), and the women would all be called Kaur (princess). Look at it from my point of view. We Hindus are all born into a caste – or out of one, in my case. Hindus marry within their caste and die within it, and people know what your caste is from your name. So if everyone had the same name, no-one could tell which caste you were from. Neat, huh?

So that's it really, the story of the birth of the Khalsa. But it doesn't answer my question. What do you think? Was it a miracle? Did Guru Gobind Rai – sorry, he's Guru Gobind Singh now – did he really chop those men's heads off and by some amazing power bring them back to life? Or was it all a clever show, a dramatic test of faith where no-one really got hurt?

Either way, you have to hand it to the Panj Piare. They believed they were going to die and still went ahead (no joke intended). What would you stick your neck out for?

ARTEFACTS IN RE:

Artefacts: Building Up a Collection. Article in *RE Today*, Autumn 1992, vol. 10, no. 1 (CEM).

Artefacts Notes, by Christine Howard (Articles of Faith). Brief guide to many of the artefacts of the world faiths: what they are, what they mean and how they are used.

Christian/Hindu/Jewish/Muslim/Sikh Artefacts Teaching Packs, by Vida Barnett (Articles of Faith). Each pack focuses on four artefacts from the religion, providing 'information tags' or background notes on the items and how they are used.

Exploring Artefacts, by Vida Barnett (Articles of Faith). An introduction for teachers. Buddhism is covered in the appendix to this booklet.

Touch and Learn: Islam/Sikhism (CEM). Two sets of handwritten worksheets, each worksheet featuring one artefact.

A Gift to the Child, by Michael Grimmitt, Julie Grove, John Hull and Louise Spencer (Simon & Schuster; available from Stanley Thornes). This package of teacher and pupil material includes some interesting ideas on using artefacts and story.

Religious Artefacts in the RE Classroom, by Paul Gateshill and Jan Thompson (Hodder & Stoughton). A guide to religious artefacts with suggestions on how they might be used.

Shropshire Education Curriculum Resources Unit have produced five books to accompany their LEA artefacts collections covering all the major world faiths except Buddhism.

STORIES:

Sunshine Religious Stories, by Owen Cole and Judith Lowndes (Heinemann). A series of twelve stories for primary pupils.

WORLD RELIGIONS:

The following are a small selection of resources teachers may find useful when planning units of work in primary RE. Books written for secondary pupils are included for *teacher reference* only.

Words and Pictures Series, by Sarah Thorley (RMEP). Five books giving basic introductions to the major world faiths for pupils aged 9–14. (Title on Buddhism in preparation.)

The Westhill Project, edited by Garth Reed, John Rudge and Geoff Teece (Stanley Thornes/Westhill College). Books for pupils aged 7–9, 9–11, 11–14, 14–16, teacher's manuals and photopacks on Christianity, Judaism and Islam, also Hinduism photopack.

Hinduism Resource Book (Westhill College). Packed with useful information for teachers and children.

Religions of the World Series (Macdonald, available from RMEP). Includes six highly illustrated books on the major world faiths for pupils aged 9–14.

Discovering Religions Series, by Sue Penney (Heinemann). Six books on the major world faiths for lower secondary pupils.

Examining Religions Series (Heinemann). Four books on Christianity, Roman Catholic Christianity, Islam and Judaism for GCSE pupils.

Living Festivals Series (RMEP). Titles on individual festivals across the six major world faiths for lower secondary pupils plus teacher's books on Christian, Hindu, Jewish and Muslim festivals. Many of the activities in the teacher's books could be used with younger pupils.

ADDRESSES:

Articles of Faith Ltd, REsource House, Kay Street, Bury BL9 6BU.

CEM (Christian Education Movement), Publications Dept, Royal Buildings, Victoria Street, Derby DE1 1GW.

Regional RE Centre (Midlands), Westhill College, Selly Oak, Birmingham B29 6LL.

INDEX

Page numbers in **bold type** indicate where terms used in several sections are explained in the text. Spellings generally follow the Glossary of Terms which accompanied the SCAA Model Syllabuses (1994).